Analysis and Presentation of Experimental Results

Analysis and Presentation of Experimental Results

R. H. Leaver
Principal Lecturer in Mechanical Engineering
Teesside Polytechnic

T. R. Thomas
Senior Lecturer in Mechanical Engineering
Teesside Polytechnic

A HALSTED PRESS BOOK

JOHN WILEY & SONS
New York

First published in the United Kingdom 1974 by
The Macmillan Press Ltd

Published in the U.S.A. by Halsted Press,
a Division of John Wiley & Sons, Inc., New York

Printed in Great Britain

Library of Congress Cataloging in Publication Data

Leaver, R   H
  Analysis and presentation of experimental results.

  "A Halsted Press book."
  Bibliography: p.
  1. Experimental design. I. Thomas, T. R., joint author. II. Title.
QA279.L38 1975   001.4'24   74–30111
ISBN 0 470–52027–2

Contents

Preface

First-degree courses in engineering and science quite rightly require a considerable portion of a student's time to be spent in the laboratory. The teaching of experimental methods is now an accepted part of many degree courses; the recently constituted C.N.A.A. degrees place particular emphasis on the importance of formal instruction in experimentation in engineering courses.

The authors have for some years been associated with a course on experimental methods for first-year students of mechanical engineering at Teesside Polytechnic. This was originally introduced into the curriculum with the object of improving the quality of presentation of course laboratory work, including a final-year research project. With due modesty we may claim to have achieved some success.

In teaching this course we were struck by the lack of guidance available to students on the analysis and presentation of experimental data. Although many excellent textbooks exist on the planning and performance of experiments, their treatment of this important topic is usually perfunctory. The required information is available but is scattered throughout books which are either too expensive or too specialised, or both, for the undergraduate reader. We felt there was a need for a textbook which would for the first time combine the most important and basic of the methods available for data presentation and analysis in a form suitable for assimilation by first-year students.

This book is largely based upon our course. Its size has been deliberately restricted so that it may be conveniently carried as a reference book to be at hand at all times. With this in mind all the tables likely to be required have been included as an appendix. These statistical tables are reproduced, with permission, from H. J. Halstead, *An Introduction to Statistical Methods,* Macmillan Company of Australia Pty. Ltd (1960). At the beginning of the book a flow diagram is given suggesting how the book may most effectively be used.

Throughout the book emphasis has been placed on methods which may be considered as tools of general utility: many of these are statistical. We take the view that, provided it is safe, these methods may legitimately be used without the necessity of a deep understanding of their mathematical derivation. This may well be considered heresy by some professional statisticians, who are generally sensitive about the possible abuse of their techniques. On the other hand most students will study statistics as a subject taught by a statistician. A little duplication is not a bad thing. A different approach to the subject can be enlightening and help to give more meaning to some of the notions when it is seen that they have useful applications. In the past, the considerable amount of repetitive arithmetic involved in statistical calculations has mitigated against their more widespread use. Nowadays most teaching establishments are equipped

with some form of computing aid and much of the drudgery of routine calculations has disappeared.

The methods described in this book (with the possible exception of
Chapter 8) could well be introduced in sixth-form colleges where much of the
habit-forming takes place. This would ease the transition into the more
sophisticated surroundings of university and polytechnic laboratories.

Finally, in all fields of engineering, deterministic methods are giving way to
stochastic treatments. The introduction of time-series analysis in Chapter 8 has
been included, not only because of its utility as an experimental tool but also
because we feel that students should develop an attitude of mind based on
probabilistic reasoning as early as possible.

Flow Charts
for Error Analysis

The three figures below suggest how the book may most effectively be used as a work of reference, to save time in finding a particular analysis. Numbers in parentheses refer to the relevant chapters.

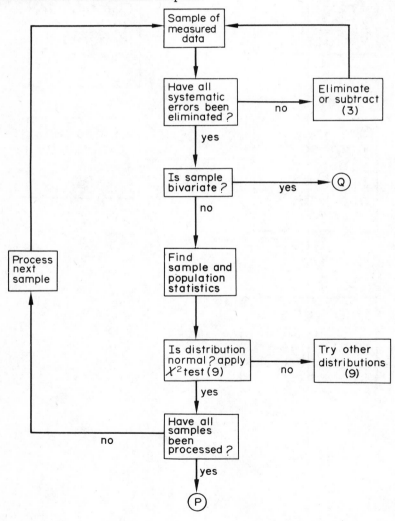

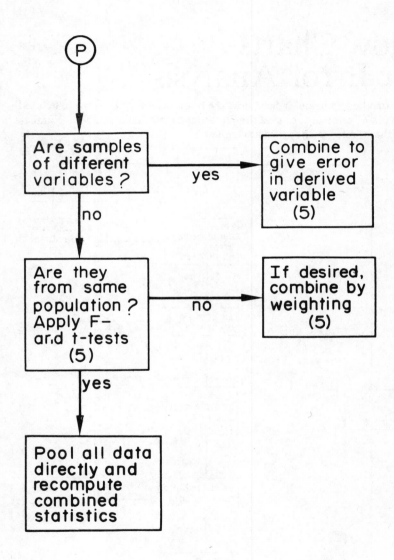

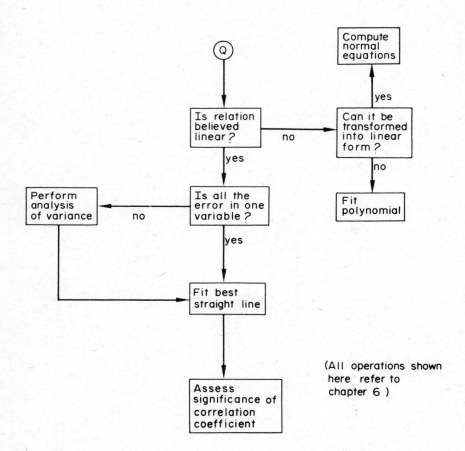

(All operations shown
here refer to
chapter 6)

1

Introduction

Engineering and the sciences are experimental disciplines. No theory, however plausible, is likely to be accepted with unqualified enthusiasm by engineers or scientists until it has been tested in the laboratory. Anyone who has studied the history of scientific discovery could not fail to be aware of the importance of the contribution to progress and discovery made by the experimentalist, from Galileo in the seventeenth century up to the present day. In every field of scientific endeavour, be it atomic physics, communications or space-flight, progress has been made only through the co-operation of the theorist with the experimentalist, and by no means least, the engineering designer. As an example of the latter, in the second half of the nineteenth century a number of physicists began independently to describe phenomena, such as electrical discharges, which led eventually to a fundamental advance in physics, the discovery of the electron. The success of their experiments depended on the production of high vacua by the mercury pump, invented by a humble German engineer in 1855. Many of the physicists concerned were quite properly rewarded with great fame and honour; the engineer was relegated to obscure textbooks on vacuum techniques. His name was Geissler. With the perspective of a century we can see that he, no less than they, was responsible for a great enlargement of human knowledge.

The supreme importance of experimentation cannot be over-emphasised. It will repay the student of any of the sciences to acquire the facility to employ the modern techniques available for the measurement of variables and the processing and analysis of data.

For our purposes we shall separate experimentation into three broad categories

(1) Design and planning

(2) Instrumentation and measurement

(3) Analysis and presentation of results

In this book we are concerned only with point 3, but this in no way minimises the importance of the other parts. Instrumentation and measurement is a vast subject in its own right. It often requires specialist knowledge and considerable practice if the user is to reach an acceptable level of proficiency. We shall not pursue the subject further here, but will refer the interested reader to the relevant literature (see recommended list of further reading).

1.1   Design and planning

It is surprising how frequently the aims of even large and elaborate experiments are poorly defined, leading to unnecessary expense and inferior results. When the precise object of an experiment is clear, a suitable procedure should be planned. This will vary with the type of experiment, but two factors, at least, always merit consideration. These are the steps required to minimise extraneous variables and the choice of suitable instrumentation to achieve the required degree of accuracy.

We shall briefly consider two examples of the kind of action which might be taken at the planning stage. It is well known that fine measurements at high resolution are easily upset by the effects of mechanical vibration and shock. Much time might be saved and frustration avoided if, at an early stage, it is decided to mount the experiment on a softly sprung base to isolate it from the effects of passing vehicles or other sources of interference.

In these days of increasing specialisation, the experimenter may be tempted, through lack of knowledge or time, to take the readings from sophisticated electronic measuring equipment on trust; this is never safe and can be embarrassing. We would not wish to argue against the benefit that this kind of equipment has brought to the laboratory, but merely point out that constant vigilance is required to ensure that the readings at the output are truly measurements of the variable. Quite simple and obvious procedures carried out before the experiment is started can save a great deal of time and wasted effort. Removal of the input signal should, of course, return the output to zero. If it does not, then clearly action is required. Assuming that the apparatus itself is sound, other causes must be sought. The intrusion of a 50 Hz ripple from the mains is not an uncommon source of trouble, or, if several pieces of equipment are being used together, a confusion in the earthing arrangements is often responsible for spurious signals. Usually the inclusion of a simple filter or a modification of the circuitry will overcome the difficulty.

This leads us to the important distinction between *systematic* and *random* errors. Systematic errors are due to some bias on the part of an instrument or an observer and can in principle be removed. They are characteristically of the same magnitude and sign. Random errors are the result of a large number of small arbitrary causes and vary both in magnitude and sign. They cannot be removed and must be treated by statistical methods.

Systematic errors can be most difficult to detect. The best insurance against them is frequent checking of the instrumentation against reliable standards, but even this is by no means foolproof. The duplication of equipment or the use of a number of independent methods of measurement is most desirable but rarely practical. The method of replication is often rewarding. The word is used to distinguish the process from mere repetition. To illustrate its application consider that during a test a reading is taken at some chosen condition. If the reading is repeated immediately it is likely there will be reasonable agreement. However, if the experimental conditions are changed and some time later the original reading is checked, agreement under these circumstances gives cause for confidence. If agreement is lacking the extraneous variable responsible must be sought and dealt with. Much may be done at the planning stage to control the influence of these disturbing effects.

Care should be exercised in selecting the order in which readings are taken. It is not difficult to imagine a situation where the effect of a slowly increasing or decreasing extraneous variable could pass unnoticed when the independent variable is regularly increased or decreased throughout a test. By changing the order of taking readings such an effect could be spread over the whole range of results and would not only be apparent but could be minimised. A satisfactory method of deciding a sequence to achieve this is to use a set of random numbers. However, if the experiment is irreversible or if an effect such as hysteresis is being studied, this technique is not helpful.

In comparative experiments where such variables as operator skill, fatigue, or time of day or night, may all produce an undesirable bias, more formal randomised block designs may be used. Advanced statistical methods exist which permit the variance of the residual bias resulting from the block design to be analysed. A considerable amount of literature is available on the subject and we shall not pursue it further.

At an early stage in planning an experiment consideration should be given to the instrumentation required. Usually several variables are to be measured. It will be shown in chapter 5 that if the dependent variable is a function of a number of measured variables, it is possible to combine the errors of measurement and to assess the weight or importance of each. In general these will not be equal and it would be prudent to exercise care in measuring the most sensitive variables, while even quite crude instrumentation may be adequate for the others.

In cases where many variables are involved the methods of dimensional analysis are useful. Suitable groups of variables may be formed, allowing the relationship between them to be displayed in a concise manner. Usually there are several possible alternative groups and a choice has to be made; this is best done at the design stage. All groups may not be equally suitable. For instance, in an experiment to investigate the viscous drag on a sphere moving through a liquid, the Reynold's number $V\rho d/\mu$ could be plotted against any of the following dimensionless groups

$$\frac{F}{V^2\rho d^2} \qquad \frac{F}{V\mu d} \qquad \frac{F\rho}{\mu^2}$$

where F is the drag force, V the velocity, d the diameter of the sphere, ρ the density of the fluid and μ the viscosity. Viscosity is very dependent on temperature and is difficult to control; hence, the greatest error is likely to be in the measurement of this variable. From this point of view it would seem sensible to arrange that the viscosity appears in one group only. Evidently therefore the best choice from the three alternatives is the first

$$\frac{F}{V^2\rho d^2}$$

When selecting instrumentation it is important to recognise the difference between precision and accuracy. Suppose that several readings of an instrument measuring a variable give a mean or average which is the true value; the instrument is said to be accurate though not necessarily precise. For example, if a pressure is known to be $100 \, \text{N/cm}^2$ and a gauge gives a series of readings of 95, 105, 90 and $110 \, \text{N/cm}^2$, the average is $100 \, \text{N/cm}^2$, an accurate value. However, if the gauge gives readings of 95, 96, 95, and $94 \, \text{N/cm}^2$, it may be said to be precise but it is certainly not accurate. A precise instrument may be used provided it is calibrated against a reliable standard, whereas one which lacks precision, or is erratic, should be discarded or repaired.

Although manufacturers of instruments usually supply information about the precision of their products their terminology is by no means standardised and may be confusing. For instance, to state that an instrument will read to within ± 5 per cent in all ranges is not, without further qualification, particularly helpful. Does the 5 per cent refer to the limits of the standard error, or the probable error, or to some other criterion? If it refers to the standard error, then 68 per cent of all readings will fall within the prescribed band, assuming that the errors are normally distributed (see chapter 4). When writing up reports the assumptions made about the precision of the instrumentation should be clearly stated. If no information is available and an estimate is made, again this must be noted. The usual estimate employed is that the maximum possible error may be plus or minus half of the least scale division of the instrument. A certain lack of precision may be tolerated and can be catered for by the statistical methods described in later chapters.

1.2   Analysis and presentation of results

A good deal of this book is about the application of statistics. There is no help for this, because statistics is the branch of mathematics by far the most helpful in the design of experiments and in the analysis of results. Most people are familiar with Churchill's famous classification of untruths into 'lies, damned lies, and statistics'. This is perhaps a little exaggerated but not entirely unfair. There is no doubt that a general lack of understanding of the subject has made it possible for the unscrupulous to manipulate and misinterpret statistical results for nefarious political and commercial ends. Why is the subject so open to abuse? Undoubtedly it largely rests on what is meant by 'proof'. Most of us first meet the word used in a Euclidian sense in geometry lessons, where we prove, for example, that two triangles are congruent and then with a satisfied flourish subscribe the work with Q.E.D. It cannot be over-emphasised, that in this sense statistics never attempts or succeeds in proving anything. However, one might put an alternative interpretation on the word. At a criminal trial, the judge may ask the jury if it is satisfied that the case has been proved beyond all reasonable doubt. Here is a notion of proof which depends upon what is meant by reasonable doubt. Much of statistics is concerned with devising ways of quantifying reasonable doubt.

In this book we shall frequently propose a hypothesis and then use statistical procedures to test the likelihood that it could be satisfied purely by chance. If we can show that this is unlikely we are inclined to accept the hypothesis, but we have proved nothing. The point is of such fundamental importance that we shall consider one further aspect of what is really the same thing. We frequently wish to determine if there is a relationship between two variables. Suppose that after plotting the results of an experiment we discover that a degree of correlation exists. It would be quite wrong to claim that this, in any way, proved a cause and effect; it most emphatically does not.

For instance, it would be easy to demonstrate a correlation of some kind between the sales figures for ladies' fur coats and the number of working-days lost in industry due to colds and influenza. No one is likely to suggest that one causes the other. In this case we know that both probably increase as winter approaches and the weather becomes inclement. However, in less obvious cases, it is all too easy to be tempted into imagining the discovery of a true cause and effect.

All this emphasises that the difficulties of statistics are not mathematical but conceptual. The algebraic manipulation needed in the subject rarely rises above the level of elementary calculus; the conceptual difficulties, however, are less trivial, and it will be worth our while to spend a little time adjusting our ideas before we begin.

A book of tables widely used by students gives the numerical value of $1/\pi$ as 0.3183 and the equatorial radius of the earth as 6378 km. When deciding how many significant figures to quote when writing a number it is conventional to truncate the number so that the last significant figure represents an error of no more than one digit. As the tabulated figures stand, therefore, they read 0.3183 ± 0.0001 and 6378 ± 1. This suggests that we know the radius of the earth almost twice as accurately as the reciprocal of π, that is, to 1 part in 3000 and to 1 part in 6000, respectively. But do we? These quantities, whose appearance and presentation in the tables is so similar, are in fact fundamentally different in kind. π or its reciprocal is a mathematical constant. It so happens that we cannot express its magnitude exactly in our system of numerical notation; nevertheless we can compute it to any desired degree of accuracy (what used to be a pastime of Victorian country parsons has since been mechanised; a computer has calculated π to 20 000 decimal places).

The radius of the earth, on the other hand, is a physical 'constant', that is to say it is not a constant at all but the result of a physical measurement. Its numerical value depends on the system of units in which it is expressed. The accuracy with which it is known depends, and depends only, on the accuracy of the experiment which measured it. There is no such thing as the exact value of a physical constant.

Students very often ask, 'But what is the *right* answer to this experiment?' This is the unfortunate result of years of conditioning, solving artificial problems in which the density of water is always exactly unity, its refractive index 4/3, and so on.

The first and most important task for the experimentalist is to jettison the mental burden of outworn determinism and to accept a much bleaker and less anthropocentric view of the universe; a reality which can only be tested by experiment, where, by Heisenberg's famous principle of uncertainty, we cannot ever in principle know the exact value of a single physical quantity. There are no right answers in science, only worse and better answers. Statistics help us choose the latter, and sometimes even get better from worse.

The basic conceptual tools of the experimentalist are those described in this book, and they are applicable whether used by a student after an hour's laboratory class or by a great research institute after ten years' work. This is what is meant by the unity of science.

Mathematicians are generally taught statistics by an approach through the theory of probability and games of chance. This is the most logical and satisfying introduction to the subject, but unfortunately not one which we have the time or space to pursue. We shall have to accept many of the basic theorems of the subject as axioms and rely heavily on physical intuition for many of our proofs. This is not necessarily a bad thing. Lawrence, one of the greatest experimental physicists of this century, knew barely enough mathematics to follow the theory of the cyclotron, but he invented it nevertheless.

Although the methods of analysis described in this book are by no means new, they have not been fully utilised either by students or mature research workers; nor have they featured large in the teaching curricula of science and engineering courses. This is understandable, for if the amount of data is considerable the drudgery involved in performing the calculations by hand can be daunting. The computer is now available, however, to deal with such repetitive work. Every experimental establishment should have readily available programs for the more frequently required calculations.

Chapter 2 is devoted to the important subject of writing reports. Scientists and engineers are often criticised for the quality of presentation of their material. It is curious that people who are prepared to take infinite pains with their work in the laboratory, often have little patience with the business of writing up the results. This is an important problem, for poor writing leads to confusion and misunderstanding; or worse, it can result in costly and even dangerous mistakes.

If communication between technical men is so difficult, how much more fraught with problems is that between the technical and non-technical. Often the layman regards the scientist with a good deal of suspicion, as a remote and perhaps rather arrogant figure with whom he has little in common. Much of the blame for this must be laid at the door of the specialist for his inability to communicate. It has been argued that the command of a subject may be measured by one's ability to explain it, particularly to the uninitiated. It is significant that many of the great men of science, both of the past and the present, have possessed this talent.

There are now many books available on the subject of report writing and others on the use of English; many are written in an entertaining style and are free of the pedantry of grammarians. In this book we can do little more than highlight the problem and offer a few simple guidelines and suggestions.

To aid the use of this book as a work of reference, a partial guide to its contents is presented in the form of flow charts (p. xi) for the treatment of experimental data, cross-referenced to appropriate chapters. We hope that this may be useful to the experimentalist in a hurry who does not have the time to work his way through chapter by chapter to seek the particular analysis he needs.

2

Report Writing

Reports may vary considerably in form depending upon the circumstances of the writer. The researcher working in a university or college will publish his findings in order to inform and, hopefully, to gain the approbation of colleagues with similar interests. In an industrial setting his work is likely to have a more restricted circulation. In all cases the prime aim of the writer should be the concise and unambiguous communication of information.

The report is the end-product of research and it is just as necessary for this to receive care and attention in its preparation as for the experimental work itself. Often the only contact between the worker and the reader is the report; years of painstaking work in the laboratory may fail to get the attention it deserves if poorly reported. The quality of the whole work will be judged largely on its presentation. A student once asked the elderly Faraday how he should go about doing research. The great man uttered three words and returned to his studies: 'Work; finish; publish'. By the last word he meant that the circulation of one's results should be treated not as an afterthought but as *an essential part* of the research.

As techniques and instrumentation become more sophisticated the cost of research increases dramatically. Indeed, in some of the more highly developed fields of aerospace the cost exceeds the financial capacity of even the largest and wealthiest of nations and is such that projects may only proceed in future as joint international ventures. The case for effective communications becomes stronger than ever.

2.1 Style and grammar

Before turning our attention to the structure and organisation of reports we shall discuss briefly a number of stylistic points which frequently give rise to confusion.

All reports must be logical and objective. It is traditional and sound that experimental work be reported dispassionately and with integrity. Within this framework the writer must attempt to be convincing and persuasive, avoiding being dull and boring. This is not an easy task and can only be achieved by a

7

great deal of practice and the study of good examples. Wide reading both within and outside the technical literature is essential. Every would-be writer should possess a good dictionary, a thesaurus and a copy of a standard work on the language.

2.1.1   Tense and voice

At one time it was conventional to adhere rigidly to the past tense, presumably because the report was often written after the experimentation was completed. Also, because it is impersonal, the passive voice was considered to be appropriate. Objectivity is of importance but it is neither necessary nor desirable to be so restricted. All the tenses may be used but care must be exercised, as unnecessary changes can be disconcerting to the reader. As a general rule tense should not be changed within a paragraph: an exception is permissible when discussing information presented in the report itself. For example, we might say: 'The graph shows that pressure increased with temperature.' To change 'increased' to 'increases' could give the impression of a generalisation which may be unwarranted.

Use of the active voice is now generally accepted and often leads to better composition with fewer grammatical errors. There need be no loss of objectivity. It is better to write 'In the second test the turbine temperature increased', rather than 'In the second test there was an increase in the turbine temperature'.

Although it should not be used too frequently, the first person plural with the active voice serves the purpose of involving the reader. We might, for instance, write 'We see that amplitude is proportional to frequency'. 'We', refers to the reader and writer. An occasional change to this tense serves to jolt the reader and hold his attention. Use of the personal pronoun 'I' is discouraged. The writer should not say 'I weighed six specimens'. The recommended form is 'Six specimens were weighed'.

2.1.2   Punctuation and paragraph structure

Each paragraph should deal with one topic only. The theme of the paragraph is introduced in the first sentence and developed or qualified in subsequent sentences. This arrangement assists the reader to follow the argument in convenient steps.

Punctuation is for the convenience of the reader. It is unnecessary to learn a set of rules; even grammarians do not appear to be universally agreed about the rules. Common sense is the best guide.

Commas should be used sparingly. If a sentence requires a number of commas placed closely together in order to make it intelligible, it could probably be improved by recasting. Care must be taken, as the sense of a phrase can be changed by the inclusion or omission of a comma.

Two sentences may be linked together by means of a semi-colon in place of a conjugation. This device often imparts greater vigour to the statement. For example, 'The strength of the material is increased; the resistance to corrosion improved'.

2.1.3 Adjectives and hyphens

The stringing together of a number of nouns to act as adjectives inhibits the smooth flow of information and is a practice to be avoided. Thus, 'Low-pressure turbine blade root loads' might be replaced by, 'Loads in the roots of the blades in the low-pressure turbine.'

Compound adjectives should be hyphenated so that the reader is in no doubt about which words are paired. For instance, 'The back pressure ball cock valve' should be written, 'The back-pressure ball-cock valve.'

A hyphen must be used if there is any possibility of a reader failing to recognise that a noun is intended to be qualified by the adjective. To write, 'The cooling water is getting warmer' is clearly nonsense. However, to the engineer the statement, 'The cooling-water is getting warmer', is quite reasonable.

2.2   The form of a report

It is not possible to set an exact form to be followed in all cases, for much will depend upon the subject reported and to whom it is addressed.

We might immediately distinguish between a record and a report. A meticulous record must be made in the laboratory of all experimental readings, serial numbers of instruments and other relevant data. Such a record is not intended for publication and may have any form that suits the experimenter. Nevertheless, it should be neat and legible so as to be useful for future reference. Memory is much too fickle to be reliable:

> He who has not made the experiment, or who is not accustomed to require rigorous accuracy from himself, will scarcely believe how much a few hours take from certainty of knowledge, and distinctness of imagery; how the succession of objects will be broken, how separate parts will be confused, and how many particular features and discriminations will be compressed and conglobated into one gross and general idea. (Johnson, *Journey to the Western Islands of Scotland*.)

A formal report can take many forms, from a comparatively short memorandum to a lengthy thesis. However, all have certain features in common and here we shall generalise.

The convenience of the reader should be the first consideration. It is usual to assume that he will have a similar intelligence and possess the same interests and background knowledge of the subject as the writer.

Any report should be structured so that it is easy to read. Headings are helpful as they break up the area of the test into digestible sections. Here is a typical, but by no means the only possible, structure.

Title
Summary or abstract
Acknowledgements
Introduction
Table of contents
List of symbols
Description of apparatus

Experimental procedure
Results
Discussion of results
Conclusions
Recommendations
References
Appendix

We shall now turn our attention to each section in turn.

2.2.1 Title

The most widely circulated part of the report will be the title. If this is not as arresting as possible few readers will ever bother to get beyond it. It must be brief and apt, so that the reader may quickly decide whether the report is of interest to him. The title should also allow the report to be correctly classified and shelved. A separate cover page may be used and should include the name of the university, research laboratory or company, and possibly an identifying number or code. If circumstances warrant it a circulation list might be added.

2.2.2 Summary or abstract

The purpose of the summary is to expand the title. It is a précis of the report and should preferably be written after the report has been completed.

As the summary is a general description of the field covered and the conclusions reached, it must be self-contained and understandable when detached from the main body of the report. Remember that this, and only this, will be carried in many of the abstracting journals and information retrieval systems. Someone who reads the abstract will need to be motivated strongly enough by it to make the effort, perhaps considerable, to look up the original article. Symbols which require reference to the report for their interpretation should not appear in the summary. New material, not covered by the report, must not be introduced. Contentious points which would turn the summary into a discussion should be omitted. Few can produce a concise and lucid summary at the first attempt. A rough draft should always be made and then pruned and polished until the most economical statement is found.

2.2.3 Acknowledgements

Acknowledgement must be made when important assistance has been obtained. It will do no harm to the writer or his work to be generous. It is correct to express appreciation of facilities which have been made available or any financial support received. Expert advice and time given to useful discussion should be recognised. It is courteous to seek permission of your assistant before recording an appreciation. After all, he may have sound reasons for not wishing to be publicly associated with the work.

2.2.4 Introduction

It may be assumed that the abstract has persuaded the reader that the report could be relevant to his interests. He will now require a little more detail. The introduction must provide this.

The first paragraph should immediately explain the particulars of the work and the method of approach. Following this, any helpful background information on the subject in general may be included. This will usually review previous work done in the field and may take the form of a short history of the subject leading up to the present problem. Consideration will have to be given to the starting point of the history and this requires judgement of the state of the reader's knowledge of the subject. References are useful and enable the reader to bring himself up to date in detail should he so wish.

2.2.5 Tables of contents

A lengthy report requires a table of contents or some form of index for the convenience of the reader. Pages must be numbered and to facilitate easy reference, the work may be divided into sections or chapters. Part of the table of contents of a research report might read:

and so on.

Of course, shorter reports which can be scanned quickly do not present a problem.

2.2.6 List of symbols

It may be satisfactory to define the meaning of symbols as they first appear in the text. For example, we might say, 'The ratio of the volume, V, of the disc, to its diameter d is given by

$$\frac{V}{d} = \frac{\pi t d}{4}$$

where t is the thickness'.

However, if the work is mathematical and requires a large number of symbols, it is also helpful to define their meaning in a separate list. Standard notation should be used where possible and may be found by reference to BS 1991.

Lengthy mathematical expressions are difficult to type and expensive to print. More importantly, they make the argument difficult to follow. A recurring form should be given an appropriate symbol. For instance, we might let

$$\phi(z) = \sin(z^2 + 1) - \cos^3 z$$

so that subsequently instead of writing out the full expression we need only use $\phi(z)$, meaning this particular function of the variable z.

2.2.7 Description of apparatus

Obviously if an item is standard and in common use then no detailed description is necessary. If the equipment embodies unusual features, the reason for their inclusion should be explained. A general description is usually given and succeeding paragraphs deal in detail with the separate parts. These paragraphs should discuss the accuracy and precision of the instruments and any calibration which may have been required.

It may well be that the first arrangement of the apparatus was less than satisfactory and modification was found to be necessary before reliable performance was obtained. Any reader, working in the same field, will value information describing this kind of development. It may prevent him from wasting a considerable amount of time by avoiding a similar pitfall.

For example, the authors recall a particular case illustrating the kind of information which is valuable. On a bearing test rig, a commercial slip-ring unit consisting of silver rings and silver–graphite brushes was used to pass signals of up to 10 mV at very small currents. The arrangement was unsatisfactory at speeds above 1000 rev/min. Eventually it was realised that the thermal voltages produced at the slip-ring contacts were of the same order of magnitude as the signal. Arrangements were made to cool the contacts with jets of air and from then on reliable readings were obtained. This kind of practical information is not readily available and increases the value and interest of a report.

A diagram or a line sketch of the apparatus is preferable to a great deal of tedious written description. Diagrams must be simple and clearly labelled. Manufacturing drawings are, as a rule, much too detailed to be easily interpreted.

Where fluid flow or electrical and electronic circuits are necessary, standard symbols must be used.

Photographs are rarely required except perhaps to illustrate relative scale or the size of the apparatus.

2.2.8 Experimental procedure

This is usually written in the past tense, and should be as brief as possible. The operation of conventional apparatus needs no comment, whereas the application of unusual equipment will require more detailed description. It is unnecessary to mention every move made in the cook-book fashion of Mrs Beeton, or to write in the style of an operator's handbook. Rather, a note should be made of the order in which readings were taken, any replication of readings and any unusual circumstances which could give rise to extraneous variables affecting the results. Where appropriate, running-in procedures and settling-times might be noted.

The design of the experiment should be discussed. It may be that the choice of variables or dimensionless groups will determine the type or accuracy of the apparatus required. Steps taken to minimise errors by special precautions or by design will be of interest.

As a general rule, the procedure should contain sufficient information to allow the reader to repeat the experiment if he so wishes.

2.2.9 Results

As most of the rest of this book is concerned with the treatment and presentation of results it is only necessary here to make a few general points.

Where applicable the results should be illustrated graphically or in tabular form. Raw experimental data must be distinguished from processed data. As we have already said, readings taken on the rig should be preserved in the worker's record book for back reference; they are not as a rule required in the report.

It is not necessary to include calculations unless some novel method has been devised, then a specimen may be presented as an appendix. Unless the report is concerned with a specialised computing problem, it is best not to include bulky computer print-out. The relevant information should be extracted and displayed concisely in a table or as a graph.

2.2.10 Discussion of results

This and the following part of the report, headed conclusions, are probably the most important sections. It is here that the results are interpreted for the reader. They may be compared with the findings of other workers or with an appropriate theory. They should be exploited to the full, but all claims must be substantiated.

When a comparison is made between theory and practice, departures, where they exist, should be mentioned and explained. It is often the departures from the expected which are the most interesting results and further our understanding of the problem.

An interesting example of this is reported by Bennett and Higginson.[1] In attempting to understand the extremely low coefficients of friction in healthy human joints (of the order 0.002) they built a very simple model consisting of a smooth rotating roller and a stationary steel plate covered with a layer of soft polythene. The two were loaded together and a lubricant was supplied by jets.

They expected low coefficients of friction down to very slow sliding speeds, and were surprised when this did not occur. It was only after completely immersing the roller and plate in the lubricant that the low coefficients of friction were achieved. However, the unexpected higher values obtained with jet lubrication had an interest of their own. It was found that they resulted from the starvation of the film at entry to the contact, which reduced the film thickness. Practically all the friction in this case arises from the shearing action in the hertzian zone. The subject of 'Starvation Lubrication' has since received a considerable amount of attention in its own right. Science advances as much by serendipity as anything else.

One of the principal aims of this book is to encourage experimenters to describe the quality of their results in clear unambiguous mathematical terms. This may be as a statement of confidence limits, a degree of correlation or, possibly, as a figure representing the goodness of fit. It follows that we deprecate, most strongly, the use of vague unquantitative phrases such as, '. . . the values obtained were fairly', 'quite' or 'reasonably good'. Or 'the length was measured accurately', or 'roughly'. Or, 'the relationship was almost linear'. All these statements are meaningless.

2.2.11 Conclusions

The conclusion summarises the discussion. It should be self-contained, as with the abstract, so that it could be read and understood even if detached from the remainder of the report. It should not include new ideas that are not covered by the report.

The O.E.D. definition of conclusion is 'ending, close, inference, final opinion'. This is applicable to the conclusion of an experimental report. It should draw inferences and close the report.

In many cases, it is fair to say that unless some conclusion has been reached, the exercise has been unsatisfactory; common sense must prevail. If the student is pressed too hard he may feel under an obligation to write something, even where there is little if anything to add to the results and the discussion. In the extreme, if the experiment consists simply of measuring a single property, and this has been quoted with its error to specified limits of confidence, there is nothing useful further to be said on the matter.

2.2.12   Recommendations

The form of the recommendations will vary with the circumstances. If the experimental work was undertaken to check the solution to a particular engineering problem, the report may result in recommending a change in component design. Such steps are often expensive and may even involve public safety and hence merit very serious consideration. It is not unknown, for example, for a motor-car manufacturer to decide, at great expense and possible damage to the company's image, to call for a modification to models already in the hands of customers. The weight of responsibility in making this kind of recommendation is clearly very great indeed.

On the other hand, in academic research the recommendations may not be so dramatic. We have already seen that research may reveal some interesting avenue, not of direct concern to the investigation in hand, but worth following up as a new project. It is appropriate to suggest new or continuing work which seems to offer promise. Research breeds further research, and in this way, usually in very small steps, our understanding is extended.

2.2.13   References

If other people's work has been mentioned, it should be listed; not only so that credit is given, but also that the reader may refer to the work for further details. If the work has been published, the reference must include:

(1)   authors' names and initials

(2)   title of paper or book

(3)   title or journal, or edition of book

(4)   volume number and possibly part number

(5)   date of publication

(6)   page number

There are two commonly used methods: the first is to give the author's name and a reference number in the text of the report. Consecutive numbers are used from the beginning of the report. For example, an author writing on jet noise might say: 'Williams, Ali and Anderson (2) have shown that a realistic value of coaxial jet attenuation is of the order of 12 to 15 dB'. The reference would then read:

(2)   T. J. Williams, M. R. Ali and J. S. Anderson, *J. Mech. Eng. Sci.*, **Vol 11**
        (No. 2), 1969, 133–42.

If the same paper or authors are mentioned again, it is not necessary to repeat
all the names; 'Williams *et al.*' will suffice.

The second method is to give the author's name and date of the publication
in the text and to list the references alphabetically. Taking our example, the
text would read: 'It has been shown that a realistic value of coaxial jet
attenuation is of the order of 12 to 15 dB (Williams, Ali and Anderson, 1969)'.
The reference would read as before but would be in its correct place alphabetically. The advantage of the second method is that should a writer wish to
include an additional reference when his report is almost completed, this is
easily done by simply inserting the name and reference. With the first method,
all reference numbers following the insertion require alteration.

2.2.14 Appendix

The function of the appendix is to present information which is relevant to the
subject and may be helpful to the reader, but if included in the main body of the
report would interfere with the smooth presentation of the material.

For instance, the appendix might include mathematical proofs or methods,
sample calculations, computer programs or flow charts.

Further work on the subject might have been completed before the report
is issued. Rather than recast the whole report, the additional material may be
added as an appendix. If a number of separate items are added as appendixes,
they should be separated and titled Appendix A, Appendix B, etc.

2.3   Specimen good and bad reports

Perhaps the easiest way of clarifying the points made in the preceding sections is
by reference to the following example. This is laid out in parallel-text form for
easier comparison of 'good' and 'bad' versions of a report of a (wholly imaginary)
experiment. The more obvious mistakes in the 'bad' version are pointed out in
footnotes, but most of the improvements in the 'good' text should be self-
explanatory.

DIMENSIONAL MEASUREMENT OF
A COPPER CYLINDER[1]

INVESTIGATION OF DIMENSIONAL
CHANGES IN A TURNED COPPER
CYLINDER

Summary

Measurements of a copper cylinder
were made. They were not all the same
size[2]. Two theories were considered
but the experimental results only
agreed with one of them[2].

Summary

Measurements of a soft copper cylinder
turned at high speed showed a significant diameter decrease at its centre,
of a magnitude in agreement with an
existing centrifugal-force theory.
Hardness measurements at each end
did not differ by an amount sufficient
to corroborate an alternative theory of
work-hardening.

1. Title not sufficiently specific. 2. Not very informative.

---

1. INTRODUCTION

A lot of people have tried to turn copper cylinders at high speed. A book about this has been written by Erstwhile (1968)[1]. Glaswegian[2] has[3] a theory that copper cylinders will narrow of their own accord. He said that if they are pure copper they will distort by centrifugal force. But Brown and other people looked at some cylinders chosen at random and they couldn't[4] see any centrifugal-force effects. In fact they made up a theory which said that sometimes they would start to work-harden at one end by themselves which would make them weak[5]. In this report I made[6] a cylinder very carefully and measured it to see if I could see anything wrong and if so which theory was the best.

1. INTRODUCTION

In recent years much attention has been given to the problem of manufacturing soft copper cylinders with particular reference to high-speed turning (Erstwhile, 1968). It has been suggested by Glaswegian (1971) that such cylinders are inherently dimensionally unstable because of surface softening due to centrifugal force. Brown *et al.* (1972), however, were not able, using visual inspection, to detect any centrifugal-force effects in a random sample of cylinders, and showed theoretically that in certain circumstances work-hardening can produce the observed effect. The present work describes an attempt to discriminate between the two theories by measurements of a test cylinder manufactured under controlled conditions.

1. Redundant sentence. 2. Undated reference. 3. Change of tense.
4. Colloquialism. 5. Which pronouns refer to what? 6. First person singular.

---

2. EXPERIMENT

I made[1] the test specimen by taking a bar of very pure copper[2] and parting off a length and mounting it in a lathe[3]. The cutting tool was changed after every 10 000 revolutions and high-flashpoint kerosene was used as a coolant as recommended by Erstwhile[4]. After machining the test specimen was placed in a prepared plastic bag in the basement of the engineering block and every effort was made to exclude sunlight and draughts by means of specially made venetian blinds[4]. It was allowed to settle for a period of 28.015 days[4]. Dimensional measurements were then made by

2. EXPERIMENT

The test cylinder was turned from stock of length 25 cm and nominal diameter 2.8 cm using standard precautions (Erstwhile, *ibid.*, p. 74). The material used was oxygen-free high-conductivity (OFHC) copper. After machining the cylinder was placed in a controlled environment and allowed to settle for about a month. Measurements were then made as follows: the diameter was measured in two directions at right angles at each end, and in four directions at 45° intervals at the centre using an optical comparator; the hardness was measured at each end at each of four stations spaced at 90°

taking the specimen and measuring its diameter in six different places at different heights[2], and then we measured[1] its hardness at eight different places[2].

round the circumference using a Vickers pyramid indenter.

1. Wrong voice and person: should be impersonal third person passive.
2. Description insufficiently specific. 3. No dimensions given. 4. Description too specific.

---

3. RESULTS AND DISCUSSION

Mostly the specimen was the same at the top and bottom but smaller round the middle. Table 1 shows the decrease in diameter[1]. The decreases were bigger than would be expected by chance[2]. They were about as big as Glaswegian[3] predicted.

The hardness seemed to be about the same[2], this is much smaller than the effect predicted by Brown and his friends[3] who supposed that this was a case of work-hardening.

3. RESULTS AND DISCUSSION

Diameters at each end were substantially the same and these (Table 1) measurements were combined to give a mean diameter of 2.8020 ± 0.0004 cm (standard error of the mean, four observations). The mean diameter at the centre, however, was 2.7893 ± 0.0009 cm (standard error of the mean, four observations). The difference of 0.0128 cm between the two sets of observations was significant at the 0.1 level (Student $t = 13.5$ with 6 degrees of freedom), and was of the order predicted by Glaswegian (*ibid.*). The mean hardnesses at each end were respectively (1305.3 ± 0.4) N/mm^2 and (1303.3 ± 0.5) N/mm^2 (standard error of the mean, four observations each). The difference of 2.0 between the two sets of observations was not significant at the 5 per cent level ($t = 2.0$ with 6 degrees of freedom), and was much smaller than that predicted by Brown *et al.* (*ibid.*) on the work-hardening hypothesis.

1. Redundant sentence. 2. Insufficiently quantitative. 3. Insufficiently specific reference.

---

4. CONCLUSIONS

The test specimen was narrower at the waist. This was not just due to chance. It was narrower by about as much as the centrifugal-force theory predicts,

4. CONCLUSIONS

The test specimen was found to have contracted significantly at the waist. The magnitude of the contraction was in good agreement with the predictions so this theory must be right. The hardness had not changed by as much as the work-hardening theory predicted so this theory must be wrong. This proves that high-speed turning is the wrong way to make copper cylinders[1].

of the centrifugal-force theory. There was no evidence, on the other hand, that the specimen had been weakened by preferential work-hardening at one end. It is therefore concluded that the centrifugal-force theory better describes the effect of high-speed turning on copper cylinders. It follows that in the present state of knowledge the use of high-speed turning for the manufacture of copper cylinders cannot be recommended without reservation.

1. Insufficiently cautious conclusions.

---

5. REFERENCES

5. REFERENCES

Erstwhile[1], (1968), *Cylinder machining*[2], Springer-Verlag, Berlin.
Glaswegian, G. G.[3] (1971), *Proc. R. Soc.* **A293**, [4].
Brown *et al.*[5] (1972), Theory and design of copper cylinder.
  Trans. ASME[6] **89F**, 477–581.

Brown, T. A., Smith, J. A. and Jones, L. (1972) Theory and design of copper cylinder. *Trans. Am. Soc. mech. Engrs* **89F**, 477–581.
Erstwhile, K. M. (1968) *Maschinen-fabriken das Cylinders,* Springer-Verlag, Berlin.
Glaswegian, G. G. (1971) Cylinder turning: towards a new theory of centrifugal-force. *Proc. R. Soc.* **A293**, 38–147.

1. Initials omitted; authors not in alphabetical order. 2. Title should be given in language of publication. 3. Title omitted. 4. Page numbers omitted. 5. All authors' names should be given in full. 6. Abbreviation is not according to *World List of Scientific Periodicals.*

Table 1[1]

Diameter at top[2]: 2.803, 2.801
Diameter at centre[2]: 2.790, 2.791, 2.789, 2.787
Diameter at bottom[2]: 2.802, 2.802
Hardness at top $\times 10^{-3}$ N/mm^2:[3] 1.303, 1.305, 1.307, 1.306
Hardness at bottom $\times 10^{-3}$ N/mm^2:[3] 1.302, 1.303, 1.304, 1.304

Table 1 **Measurements of diameter and indentation hardness**

Diameter at top (cm): 2.803, 2.801
Diameter at centre (cm): 2.790, 2.791, 2.789, 2.787
Diameter at bottom (cm): 2.802, 2.802
Hardness at chuck end (N/mm^2): 1.303, 1.305, 1.307, 1.306 $\times 10^3$
Hardness at other end (N/mm^2): 1.302, 1.303, 1.304, 1.304 $\times 10^3$

1. No title. 2. No units. 3. Ambiguous: is hardness 10^{-3} times tabulated figures or vice versa?

3

Some Statistical Ideas

Qualitative experimental work results in data consisting of measurements, using the term in its broadest sense.

The variable measured may either be *continuous,* in that it may take any value, within the limits of precision of the apparatus employed, or it may be *discrete* if determined merely by counting.

For example an observer, in attempting to establish a true length, may take a number of measurements with a metre-rule and find that they differ by small amounts. This set of measurements form a sample of a continuous variate. It would be unwise to record the results with greater precision than 0.5 mm. Setting aside this limitation, it is not difficult to imagine readings in this case taking values from far below to well above the true length in a continuous fashion.

Alternatively, in an experiment concerned with the number of defective components produced in a shift from a particular machine, the variate will be an integer resulting from counting the components. If the experiment continues over several shifts a sample of a discrete variable will result.

As the sample size is increased, we feel intuitively that the additional information will, in the first case, allow a better estimate of the true length to be made and in the second case, give a clearer picture of the distribution of the numbers of defective parts.

3.1 The histogram

The usual and most satisfactory method of illustrating the distribution of a variate is by means of a histogram. This diagram is arranged as shown in figure 3.1 with the values of the variate plotted horizontally and the areas of the rectangles representing the frequency with which the variate occurs. The ordinates are measures of frequency density. If the variate is discrete the rectangles are constructed with the value of the variate at the mid-point of the base of each rectangle. If the variate is continuous it is necessary to group the results before constructing the histogram. The width of the rectangles is arbitrary and some skill and experience is required in making a suitable choice.

19

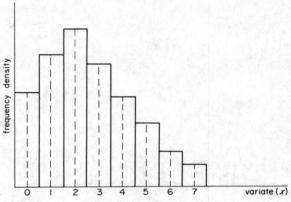

Figure 3.1. Typical histogram.

If the width is either too small or too great, the form of the distribution may be obscured. Care must be exercised to avoid ambiguity if the value of a variate coincides with a class boundary; the situation is best avoided.

Although the histogram is a convenient representation, some information is lost in grouping, since all variates within a class are assumed to take the central value.

3.2   Frequency and probability distributions

As the sample size of a continuous variate is increased, the class width may be reduced while the frequency density remains substantially unchanged. Carried to the limit the outline of the histogram becomes a smooth curve, as in figure 3.2, representing the frequency distribution of the population.

It will be adequate for our purposes to define probability as the ratio of successful outcomes to the total number of possible outcomes of an event.

$$\text{Probability} = \frac{\text{Successful outcomes}}{\text{Total possible outcomes}} \tag{3.1}$$

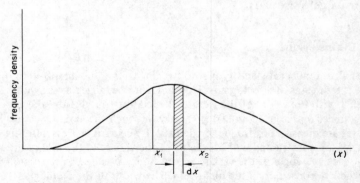

Figure 3.2. Typical frequency distribution.

For instance, if a coin is tossed the outcome may either be a head or a tail. If a head is regarded as a success, then the probability of a toss resulting in a success is 0.5. The probability of a success or a failure is of course 1.0. If the experiment was performed a number of times we would not expect exactly half the tosses to be heads. However, as the number of tosses increased we would expect this to become more nearly true.

Now returning to the frequency-distribution diagram for a population; if the scales are suitably adjusted so that the area under the curve is made equal to unity, the diagram may be considered to represent the *probability distribution* of all possible outcomes of an event.

The idea of the probability distribution seems to have been first used in the eighteenth century in a study of the theory of errors of observation, by Simpson (according to Whittaker and Robinson) who assumed a theoretical distribution in the form of an isosceles triangle, negative errors being as likely as positive. Errors outside the triangle were considered impossible. A more usual and useful bell-shaped distribution of errors attributed to Gauss is considered in detail in chapter 4.

As the area of the diagram represents probability the curve may be expressed as a function of the variate, say x, and the ordinates are measures of *probability density* denoted by $p(x)$.

Clearly the probability of x falling between x_1 and x_2 is given by

$$\text{Probability } (x_1 < x < x_2) = \int_{x_1}^{x_2} p(x)\, dx \tag{3.2}$$

also by definition

$$\text{Probability } (-\infty < x < \infty) = \int_{-\infty}^{\infty} p(x)\, dx = 1 \tag{3.3}$$

We may define a further useful function, the *cumulative probability* $P(x)$. This is the probability that x will be less than or equal to x_1. That is to say

$$\text{Probability } (x < x_1) = \int_{-\infty}^{x_1} p(x)\, dx = P(x_1) \tag{3.4}$$

It is evident that

$$p(x) = (d/dx) P(x) \tag{3.5}$$

and

$$P(x < \infty) = \int_{-\infty}^{\infty} p(x)\, dx = 1 \tag{3.6}$$

That is to say, that $P(x_1)$ represents the area of the probability distribution diagram to the left of the value of the variate x_1 being considered. A typical cumulative-probability curve is shown in figure 3.3.

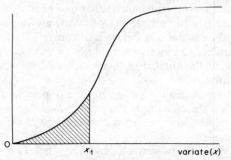

Figure 3.3. Typical cumulative.probability curve.

3.3   Moments of the probability-density distribution for a population

The moment of a distribution about any origin is defined as

$$\mu_r = \int_{-\infty}^{\infty} g^r(x)\, p(x)\, dx \tag{3.7}$$

where $g(x)$ is any chosen function of x.

3.3.1   First moment

If $g(x)$ is simply x, we have the first moment of the distribution, and

$$\mu_r = \mu_1 = \mu$$

is the mean value of x, of the population; so that

$$\mu = \int_{-\infty}^{\infty} xp(x)\, dx \tag{3.8}$$

(see figure 3.4).

An analogy due to Crandall, which is helpful to engineers, is to compare the probability distribution with a horizontal rod of variable mass density as shown in figure 3.5. The probability density $p(x)$ and mass density $p(x)$ are analogues and the first moment about the origin gives the mean value of the

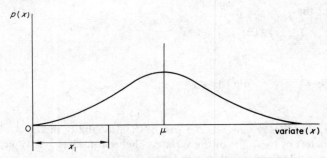

Figure 3.4. First moment of probability distribution about origin.

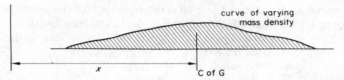

Figure 3.5. Mass–density analogue of probability distribution.

variate on the one hand, and the position of the centres of gravity of the rod, on the other.

μ is also called the expectation of x, that is, $E(x)$.

Suppose we are owed £50 by an unreliable person and we have only a 50 per cent chance of repayment. We are also owed £25 by a second, rather dishonest person, and have only a 10 per cent chance of seeing the money again. Unlike Mr Micawber, we may, at least statistically be clear about our expectations.

$$E(x) = (£50 \times 0.5) + (£25 \times 0.1)$$
$$= £27.50$$

We expect a return of £27.50.

3.3.2 Second moment

If $g(x)$ is made equal to x^2, then

$$\mu_2 = \int_{-\infty}^{\infty} x^2 p(x)\, dx \tag{3.9}$$

This is the second moment about the chosen origin and is analogous to the moment of inertia of the rod about the origin.

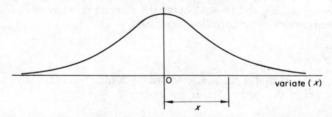

Figure 3.6. Probability distribution of figure 3.4 with origin referred to the mean.

If x is measured from the mean (μ) as in figure 3.6 then μ_2 is called the variance of the population and is denoted by σ^2.

$$\sigma^2 = \int_{-\infty}^{\infty} (x - \mu)^2 p(x)\, dx$$

$$= \int_{-\infty}^{\infty} x^2 p(x) - 2\mu \int_{-\infty}^{\infty} xp(x)\, dx + \mu^2 \int_{-\infty}^{\infty} p(x)\, dx$$

$$= \mu_2 - 2\mu^2 + \mu^2 \tag{3.10}$$

or

$$\sigma^2 = \mu_2 - \mu^2 \tag{3.11}$$

Returning to our analogue, this equation is the equivalent of the parallel-axis theorem for moments of inertia; where σ^2 is analogous to the moment of inertia about the centre of gravity and μ_2 is, as in equation 3.9, equivalent to the moment of inertia about the origin.

If x is measured from the mean, and $\mu = 0$, then

$$\sigma^2 = \mu_2 = \int_{-\infty}^{\infty} x^2 p(x)\, dx \tag{3.12}$$

Clearly, the variance is a measure of the spread or dispersion of the variate about the mean of the distribution.

Higher moments than the second have a limited use in describing the shape of the distribution, but will not be considered here.

3.4   The calculation of sample parameters

3.4.1   Measures of central tendency

3.4.1.1   The mode

The mode is the value of the variate which occurs with the greatest frequency. It may not exist, or may not be unique. It is not a convenient parameter and has limited use.

3.4.1.2   The median

If the values of the variate are arranged in an array, the median is the middle value, or the arithmetic mean of the two middle values. The median divides the histogram into two equal parts. The values which divide the histogram into four parts are called quartiles, and those dividing the diagram into ten and a hundred parts are called deciles and percentiles respectively.

3.4.1.3   The mean

The mean is the most useful parameter describing central tendency, and is simply the average value of the variate, and is denoted by $\bar{x}$.

$$\bar{x} = \sum_{i=1}^{n} x_i/n \tag{3.13}$$

or more briefly,

$$\bar{x} = \Sigma\, x/n$$

where n is the number of values of the variate in the sample.

For grouped data, or if the values of the variate are repeated, a more convenient form is

$$\bar{x} = \Sigma fx/\Sigma f \tag{3.14}$$

where f is the frequency with which x occurs in the group.

3.4.2 Measures of dispersion

The mean does not tell us anything about the precision of our measurements. Consider, for instance, the two sets of weighings in table 3.1. They have the same mean, but even by casual inspection the variation in the first set is much greater than that in the second. We need a means of quantifying this variation.

Table 3.1. Two sets of weighings with the same mean but different variances

Set A x grammes	Set B x grammes
20.48	26.11
26.62	26.12
18.73	26.11
28.61	26.20
34.32	26.16
27.14	26.20
30.09	26.12
23.23	26.20
$\Sigma x = 209.22$	$\Sigma x = 209.22$
$\bar{x} = 26.1525$	$\bar{x} = 26.1525$

3.4.2.1 Range

The range is the difference between the largest and smallest values of the variate.

3.4.2.2 Mean deviation

The mean deviation is given by

$$\Sigma\,(x-\bar{x})/n \qquad (3.15)$$

3.4.2.3. Standard deviation

This is the most useful of the measures of dispersion and is defined by

$$s^2 = \frac{\Sigma\,(x-\bar{x})^2}{n} \qquad (3.16)$$

or, if the data is grouped, as

$$s^2 = \frac{\Sigma f(x-\bar{x})^2}{\Sigma f} \qquad (3.17)$$

where s is the standard deviation of the sample and s^2 the variance of the sample.

3.4.3   *Calculation of standard deviation*

The practical calculation of standard deviation looks at first sight rather tedious. It appears that we first have to find the mean, then square all the individual differences from the mean and add them. However, we can avoid a lot of this work by a little algebraic manipulation.

These expressions may be recast into a more convenient form for calculation.

$$\Sigma (x - \bar{x})^2 = \Sigma x^2 + n\bar{x}^2 - 2\bar{x} \Sigma x$$

substituting $n\bar{x}$ for Σx

$$\Sigma (x - \bar{x})^2 = \Sigma x^2 + n\bar{x}^2 - 2n\bar{x}^2$$

Therefore

$$s^2 = \frac{\Sigma x^2}{n} - \bar{x}^2 \tag{3.18}$$

Alternatively, for grouped data

$$s^2 = \frac{\Sigma fx^2}{\Sigma f} - \bar{x}^2 \tag{3.19}$$

Note the similarity of form between this equation and that for the variance of the population.

Table 3.2 shows the working of the problem using this method. It also discloses a severe drawback. To obtain the standard deviation correct to three significant figures it is necessary to perform calculations with eight significant

Table 3.2. Computation of variances and standard deviations for the data of table 3.1 using equation 3.18

Set A		Set B	
x	x^2	x	x^2
20.48	419.4304	26.11	681.7321
26.62	708.6244	26.12	682.2544
18.73	350.8129	26.11	681.7321
28.61	818.5321	26.20	686.4400
34.32	1177.8624	26.16	684.3456
27.14	736.5796	26.20	686.4400
30.09	905.4081	26.12	682.2544
23.23	539.6329	26.20	686.4400
$\Sigma x = 209.22$	$\Sigma x^2 = 5656.8828$	$\Sigma x = 209.22$	$\Sigma x^2 = 5471.6386$

$\bar{x}^2$	= 683.9533	$\bar{x}^2$	= 683.9533
$\Sigma x^2/n$	= 707.1103	$\Sigma x^2/n$	= 683.9548
s^2	= 707.1103 − 683.9533	s^2	= 683.9548 − 683.9533
	= 23.1570		= 0.0015
s	= 4.81	s	= 0.04

figures. This is because $n\Sigma x^2 - (\Sigma x)^2$ is a small difference between two large numbers, a situation always to be avoided where possible.

This would be a tedious computation with a desk calculator and laborious by hand. If n was 100 instead of 8 the labour hardly bears imagining and could not be performed without a mistake. Need we worry when computers are readily available? Unfortunately yes; most of the current generation of computers will only calculate to eleven significant figures and if our data exceeded a few hundred numbers they would infallibly return a wrong answer.

Fortunately we can use another simple ruse to get around this difficulty. This uses the concept of a *fictitious mean*.

We choose some convenient arbitrary value, say the middle reading, as our fictitious mean x_o, and we choose a convenient arbitrary multiplier c such that

$$x_i = x_o + ct_i \tag{3.20}$$

t_i is the new variable with which we will perform the calculations. Equations 3.13 and 3.28 become with a little manipulation

$$\bar{x} = x_o + c\Sigma t/n \tag{3.21}$$

(or for grouped data $\bar{x} = \Sigma fx_o/\Sigma f + c\Sigma ft/\Sigma f$)

$$\bar{x} = x_o + c\bar{t} \tag{3.22}$$

where $\bar{t}$ is the mean of the variable t and

$$s^2 = c^2\left[\frac{\Sigma t^2}{n} - \left(\frac{\Sigma t}{n}\right)^2\right] \tag{3.23}$$

or for grouped data

$$s^2 = c^2\left[\frac{\Sigma ft^2}{\Sigma f} - \left(\frac{\Sigma t}{n}\right)^2\right] \tag{3.24}$$

The first set of results of tables 3.1 and 3.2 are reworked in table 3.3.to show the advantage of this method, using $x_o = 26.12$ and $c = 1/100$.

Note that an error of any kind should be quoted to two significant figures, and the result which it qualifies should then be written to a corresponding number of decimal places. This convention will be maintained throughout the book. Thus the statistics calculated for the two sets of data of table 3.1 should be presented respectively as 26.2 ± 4.8 g (standard deviation, eight observations) and 26.153 ± 0.040 g (standard deviation, eight observations).

Note also that the actual figures must always be qualified in *three* ways: by the units of measurement; by the name of the statistic; and by the number of observations. (Any statistical parameter is called a statistic in the technical literature.) The reason for the first qualification should be self-evident. The reasons for the second two are that, as we shall see shortly, the standard deviation is by no means the only statistic which can express precision, and the importance to be attached to any statistic depends on the number of observations used in computing it.

Table 3.3. Computation of mean, variance and standard deviation using fictitious mean, equations 3.21 and 3.23. $x_o = 26.12$ g, $c = 0.01$

x	t	t^2
26.11	−1	1
26.12	0	0
26.11	−1	1
26.20	8	64
26.16	4	16
26.20	8	64
26.12	0	0
26.20	8	64
$\Sigma t = 26$	$\Sigma t^2 = 210$	$\Sigma t/n = 3.25$

$$\bar{x} = 26.12 + 0.01 \times 3.25 = 26.1525$$
$$s^2 = 0.01^2(210/8 - 3.25^2)$$
$$= 0.00156875 \text{ g}^2$$
$$s = 0.040 \text{ g}$$

3.5   Sample and population properties

The distinction between sample properties and population properties is so important that separate sets of symbols are generally used, lower-case Roman for samples and lower-case Greek for the population.

$\bar{x}$ = mean of sample
s^2 = variance of sample
μ = mean of population
σ^2 = variance of population

3.5.1   *Best estimates of population parameters*

We shall assume when dealing with experimental observations that the best estimate of the mean of the population is the mean of the sample. That is

$$\mu_e = \bar{x}$$

This is a postulate which stems from the classic work of Gauss, and has received a great deal of attention since that time; in rare instances it may fail. However, it will serve our purpose.

Further, we shall accept that the variance of the sample s^2 underestimates the variance of the population. To correct this the variance will be multiplied by the so-called Bessel correction, $n/(n-1)$, where n is the number of observations in the sample.

$$\sigma_e^2 = s^2(n/(n-1)) \tag{3.25}$$

Note that as the sample size increases this factor approaches unity.

An alternative view is to regard the denominator $(n - 1)$ as the 'degrees of freedom' of the problem. We have already calculated the mean and hence placed a restriction on the deviations, reducing the degrees of freedom by one. Therefore the remaining degrees of freedom are $(n - 1)$.

Hereafter we shall drop the subscript e. This was introduced to serve as a reminder that we can never know the true population parameters. All we may do is make a best estimate.

3.5.2 Sheppard's correction

The variance calculated from grouped data may be improved by applying Sheppard's correction.

corrected variance = (calculated variance from grouped data)

$$= -c^2/12$$

where c is the class interval.

The method may be extended to the calculation of higher moments. The correction must be used with care as it only really applies to cases where the frequency curve has long low tails at each end, and where the curve may reasonably be approximated by a series of trapezoids.

4

Normal Distribution

There are many different frequency distributions in statistics, some of which we shall meet later in the book, but one in particular applies to the theory of errors. This is the *normal* or *Gaussian* distribution. The word 'normal' is here used in its original sense of 'ideal', for it was believed for a long time that this distribution was a reflection of a universal and fundamental law of nature. If certain assumptions are made it can be 'proved' that the accumulation of a large number of small independent random deviations follows a normal law, but belief in the rigour of this proof is no longer widespread. There is a well-known quotation on the subject: 'Everybody believes in the Gaussian law of errors; the experimenters because they think it will be proved by mathematics; and the mathematicians because they believe it has been established by observation.' However, for our present purposes we can assume that the Gaussian distribution is the best possible representation of the variation of small random errors.

4.1 Properties

The first appearance of the normal distribution function $p(x)$ is rather forbidding

$$p(x) = \frac{1}{\sigma(2\pi)^{1/2}} \exp\left\{-\frac{(x-\mu)^2}{2\sigma^2}\right\} \tag{4.1}$$

Common sense leads us to expect that the effect of a large number of small positive deviations from the mean should be similar to that of the same number of negative deviations, and indeed the term in $(x - \mu)^2$ ensures that the distribution is symmetrical about the mean (figure 4.1a).

It is interesting to reflect that this curve lay unnoticed for millennia literally under the feet of the human race until Gauss brought it to our attention; inverted and with the horizontal scale expanded, it is of course the contour of the edges of every old flight of stone steps, worn in the centre more than the outside.

Figure 4.2a shows an interesting example from modern engineering practice: the distribution of heights along a section of a ground surface.

30

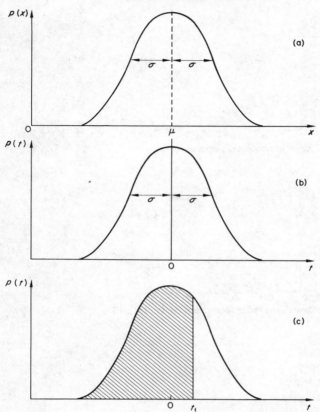

Figure 4.1. (a) Normal (Gaussian) frequency distribution. (b) Normal frequency distribution with origin referred to population mean. (c) Shaded area represents the probability that $t < t_1$.

In equation 4.1 we have three variables to handle simultaneously; x, μ and σ. We can recast the expression in a much more general form by writing

$$t = (x - \mu)/\sigma \qquad (4.2)$$

The new variable t is *dimensionless*, because x, μ and σ are always in the same units. If we replot figure 4.1a with t as ordinate we see the new mean has shifted to zero (figure 4.1b). We write

$$p(t) = (1/\sigma(2\pi)^{1/2}) \, \exp\left(\frac{-t^2}{2}\right) \qquad (4.3)$$

where $p(t)$ is the *probability density* and is simply the value of the ordinate of the Gaussian curve corresponding to an abscissa of value t. To obtain a probability we must find the area under some portion of the curve. The probability that a given value of t will lie between any two values t_1 and t_2

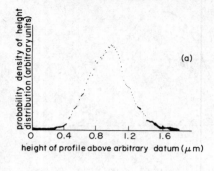

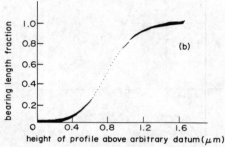

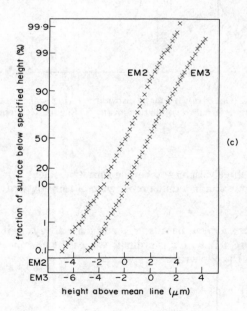

Figure 4.2. (a) Gaussian height distribution on a ground surface[2]. (b) Cumulative distribution of (a)[2]. (c) Cumulative height distribution for two bead-blasted surfaces, plotted on a normal probability scale[3].

must be the ratio of the area under the curve between t_1 and t_2 to the total area under the curve, that is

$$\text{Prob}\,(t_1 < t < t_2) = \int_{t_1}^{t_2} p(t)\,dt \Big/ \int_{-\infty}^{\infty} p(t)\,dt \tag{4.4}$$

but the total area under the curve represents the probability that t will lie between ∞ and $-\infty$. Of course, this probability must be unity, so

$$\text{Prob}\,(t_1 < t < t_2) = \int_{t_1}^{t_2} p(t)\,dt \tag{4.5}$$

Now by the usual rules of integration

$$\int_{t_1}^{t_2} p(t)\,dt = \int_{-\infty}^{t_2} p(t)\,dt - \int_{-\infty}^{t_1} p(t)\,dt \tag{4.6}$$

$\int_{-\infty}^{t_1} p(t)\,dt$ is written as $P(t_1)$ and is called the *cumulative normal-distribution function*. It is the area under the curve from $-\infty$ to t_1 and thus represents the probability that t is less than t_1 (figure 4.1c), that is

$$P(t_1) = \text{Prob}\,(t < t_1) \tag{4.7}$$

Every book of statistical tables lists a range of values of $p(t)$ and $P(t)$, or of similar functions. These tables have unit standard deviation and hence can be applied to a distribution of any variation. Then equation 4.5 becomes

$$\text{Prob}\,(t_1 < t < t_2) = P(t_2) - P(t_1) \tag{4.8}$$

and we can find this probability instantly simply by looking up the two values of $P(t)$ in the table and subtracting them.

Table 4.1 lists a few important values of $P(t)$. (We shall not often need values of the probability density $p(t)$.) We can deduce some very interesting limits for our experimental results at a glance. Two-thirds of all the results we could measure would lie within one standard deviation of the mean (that is, $t = \pm 1$); 95 per cent would lie within two standard deviations, while no less than 99.5 per cent would lie within ± 3. To put this another way, only five measurements in every thousand would lie more than three standard deviations from the mean of a normal distribution.

Table 4.1. Important values of t and $P(t) = \int_{-\infty}^{t} p(t)\,dt$

t	$P(t)$
-1	0.159
0	0.500
1	0.841
2	0.977
3	0.9987
-2.33	0.01
-1.64	0.05
-0.675	0.25
0.675	0.75
1.64	0.95

A parameter much used by experimenters, though disliked by statisticians, is the *probable error*. This defines the limits within which half the experimental errors will lie, and turns out to be about $2\sigma/3$ from the mean (actually 0.6745).

4.2   Application

Let us see how these properties of the normal distribution can be put to practical use. Consider the case of the owner of a mobile hot-dog stand waiting outside a football match. In calculating his season's operating strategy it is important that he knows the average finishing time of the match. If he cooks his hot dogs a fraction too early he will find himself selling overcooked sausages; if a fraction too late he will build up a queue a hundred yards long. In either event he risks his stand being overturned by infuriated customers.

Football matches these days generally run into injury time, and the length of injury time, being due to random factors, will be normally distributed about a mean. Suppose this mean is known to be 6.8 minutes with a standard deviation of 2.2 minutes. Then our hot-dog seller can tell immediately that half of all matches run over time by between 5.3 and 8.3 minutes, that is, by $6.8 \pm (2.2 \times 2/3)$ minutes. He can tell further than 2/3 of all matches run over by between 4.6 and 9 minutes, that is, 6.8 ± 2.2 minutes, and that nineteen matches out of twenty (95 per cent) end between 2.4 and 11.2 minutes late (that is, $6.8 \pm 2 \times 2.2$).

How many matches end within a minute after the mean length of injury time? From equation 4.2

$$t = 1/2.2 = 0.455$$

Entering the tables for $P(0.455)$, we find that the answer is 0.6754 or 67.5 per cent. If we want the proportion of matches ending within a minute either way of the mean time, it is simply $(0.6754 - 1/2) \times 2 = 0.3508$ or 35.1 per cent.

Experience has taught our street merchant that if the match ends more than twelve minutes late the destruction of his property is certain. How often is this likely to occur? Equation 4.2 gives us

$$t = (12 - 6.8)/2.2 = 2.36$$

Entering the tables for $P(2.36)$ gives us 0.99086. The figure we want, of course, is $1 - P(t) = 0.00914$ or 0.9 per cent. Thus the chance of catastrophe is less than one in a hundred and our hero should be safe for several seasons.

It is often convenient to plot the cumulative probability function directly against t. For a normal distribution this gives a characteristic S-shaped or ogival curve (figure 4.2b). $P(t)$ may also be plotted on a special scale distorted so that a normally distributed variate yields a straight line (figure 4.2c). This is a useful rapid test for normality.

It is necessary to warn here against a possible source of confusion. Many writers follow the definition of $P(t)$ which we have just given. Many others, however, do not, and there are almost as many different forms of tables as there are statisticians. Fortunately it is quite easy to convert from one to the other. The most common variation is to change the limits of integration; thus some tables integrate from 0 to t while others integrate from $-t$ to t. As

$$\int_{-\infty}^{0} p(t)\, dt = \int_{0}^{\infty} p(t)\, dt = 1/2 \tag{4.9}$$

so

$$\int_{0}^{t} p(t)\, dt = \int_{-\infty}^{t} p(t)\, dt = -1/2 \tag{4.10}$$

This disposes simply of the first variation; the second variation is dealt with just as easily if we remember that by symmetry

$$\int_{-t}^{t} p(t)\, dt = 2\int_{0}^{t} p(t)\, dt \tag{4.11}$$

A slightly more difficult problem is set by some writers' use of the *error function*.

This is defined as

$$\text{erf}\,(t/(2)^{1/2}) = \frac{2}{(\pi)^{1/2}} \int_{0}^{t/(2)^{1/2}} \exp\,(-s^2)\, ds$$

It is related to $P(t)$ by

$$2P(t) = \text{erf}\,(t/(2)^{1/2}) + 1$$

As statisticians rarely use it anyway it hardly seems worth the trouble. The best rule is to stick to the same book of tables for all calculations, and if you must use a strange book inspect the table heading carefully.

Some authors also include tables of $1 - P(t)$, which are very useful for people unable to perform subtraction.

We have thus seen two ways of expressing the precision of a set of data, the standard deviation and the probable error. There is a third precision index which is used more widely than either of the others; this is called the standard error of the mean.

Table 4.2. Some commonly used precision indices applied to the results of table 3.1

	Set A	Set B
Standard deviation of sample	4.81	0.040
Probable error of sample	3.24	0.027
Standard error of mean	1.94	0.011
Probable error of mean	1.31	0.007
95 per cent confidence limits of mean	3.89	0.022

We have already discussed the difference between sample mean and population mean. If from the same population we take a large number of samples or sets of observations, each containing n values, it is intuitively reasonable that the means of these samples will form a distribution of their own, and that the mean of this distribution will be the mean μ of the population. It can be shown that this is indeed so, and that the distribution of sample means is itself normal. Moreover, it remains quite closely normal even if the population is quite badly skewed. The standard deviation σ_m of this distribution of means is $\sigma/(n)^{1/2}$, and hence we may write it down in terms of the sample standard deviation as

$$\sigma_m = s/(n-1)^{1/2} \tag{4.12}$$

This so-called standard error of the mean is strictly the error in μ, not in $\bar{x}$. However, we have already seen that the sample mean is the best estimate of the population mean.

Equation 4.12 leads us to deduce that attempts to improve the precision by increasing the sample size are subject to the law of diminishing returns. Taking, say, 100 measurements instead of 10 will give us not 10 times the precision but $(99/9)^{1/2} = 3.3$ times only for the estimated population standard deviation.

The results of table 3.2 can now be presented as 26.2 ± 1.8 g and 26.152 ± 0.015 g respectively (standard error of the mean, eight observations) or as 26.2 ± 1.2 g and 26.152 ± 0.010 g respectively (probable error of the mean, eight observations). This is a notable increase in precision for a little extra arithmetic.

This is an appropriate point to consider the problem of a sample which contains an observation deviating so markedly from the mean that it produces a disproportionate increase in the calculated error. Assuming that no experimental evidence can be found for doubting the accuracy of the observation, is it ever permissible to reject it so as to improve the overall precision of the results?

In fact a number of statistical criteria have been proposed on which such an observation may be rejected. Of these the most widely used is *Chauvenet's criterion*. This is defined such that the probability of an observation lying outside the set limits $\pm t_{ch}$ is $1/2n$, that is, the criterion is a function of the sample size. Thus

$$\text{Prob}\,(\,|t| > |t_{ch}|\,) = 1/2n$$

This is the sum of upper and lower tails of the distribution

$$P(-t_{ch}) + \{1 - P(t_{ch})\} = 1/2n$$

By symmetry

$$P(-t_{ch}) = 1 - P(t_{ch})$$

so finally

$$P(t_{ch}) = 1 - 1/4n$$

The criterion becomes more difficult to satisfy as n increases (figure 4.3), until for very large samples the probability of rejecting an observation is very small indeed; this is in accord with common sense.

The sample statistics should then be recomputed without the rejected observations and, strictly, Chauvenet's criterion should again be applied to the new figures. In practice, however, if out of a sample of a dozen or so measurements more than one has to be rejected, then the probability is either that the experimental technique is defective or that the parent population is not normally

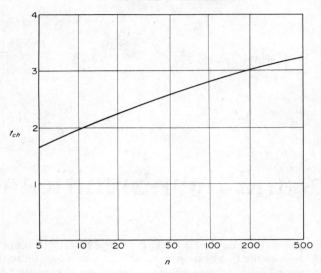

Figure 4.3. Chauvenet's criterion as a function of sample size.

distributed. It would be sensible in the circumstances to apply a chi-squared test
as described in chapter 9.

It is important to remember that Chauvenet's criterion does not 'prove'
that an observation is defective. It and all other statistical criteria are arbitrary
by definition and are merely conventions which a body of scientists have agreed
to accept. A small but finite number of observations will always be out of line
for perfectly genuine reasons, and someone has to suffer them just to keep the
books of the universe straight. If in doubt use common sense — but if you decide
to reject a doubtful observation, *always* record the details in your final report
so others can make up their own minds about it.

5

Errors and their Significance

In practical experimentation our data is rarely contained in a single sample. Very commonly we measure two or more variables, each with its own sources of error, and need to combine our measurements in some way so as to find the resultant error in some other derived variable. Again, we may have a number of samples of measurements of the same variable; under what circumstances may we pool our results, and if this proves not to be permissible how else may we combine the measurements? Finally, we may need to know whether the parameter we are measuring has suffered some change due to a change in experimental conditions; we thus seek to develop quantitative tests which will establish a balance of probability.

5.1   Combination of errors

In the familiar simple pendulum experiment the period of oscillation T is related to the length L by

$$T = 2\pi(L/g)^{1/2}$$

Thus when this experiment is used to calculate the gravitational acceleration we have

$$g = 4\pi^2 L/T^2 \tag{5.1}$$

In other words, to determine g we need to measure both the length of the pendulum and its period. Each of these measurements is itself susceptible to error. How do we combine the errors in our estimate of g?

Let us look at the general case of a derived quantity u which is some function of two independent variables x and y, that is

$$u = f(x, y)$$

Now $u_i = \bar{u} + \delta u_i$, $x_i = \bar{x} + \delta x_i$, $y_i = \bar{y} + \delta y_i$ where the delta is used to indicate a residual. So

$$\bar{u} + \delta u = f(\bar{x} + \delta x, \bar{y} + \delta y)$$

If this is expanded in a Taylor series we obtain

$$\bar{u} + \delta u = f(\bar{x}, \bar{y}) + \frac{\partial u}{\partial x} \delta x + \frac{\partial u}{\partial y} \delta y + \text{higher terms}$$

We can replace $f(\bar{x}, \bar{y})$ by $\bar{u}$ and remove it from both sides, leaving us (neglecting higher terms) with

$$\delta u = \frac{\partial u}{\partial x} \delta x + \frac{\partial u}{\partial y} \delta y \tag{5.2}$$

Equation 5.2 can be extended to include any number of variables. Applying it to equation 5.1

$$\delta g = \frac{\partial g}{\partial L} \delta L + \frac{\partial g}{\partial T} \delta T$$

$$= \frac{4\pi^2}{T^2} \delta L + \left(-\frac{2}{T^3}\right) 4\pi^2 L \delta T$$

As the sign of an individual residual is not known, the worst possible case is always taken in which residuals are presumed to be of the same sign. Remembering this and rearranging

$$\delta g = \frac{4\pi^2 L}{T^2} \frac{\delta L}{L} + \frac{4\pi^2 L}{T^2} \frac{2\delta T}{T}$$

Dividing through by $g = 4\pi^2 L / T^2$

$$\frac{\delta g}{g} = \frac{\delta L}{L} + \frac{2\delta T}{T} \tag{5.3}$$

You may well have been taught a rule-of-thumb procedure for combining errors in which proportional errors are multiplied by the power to which their parent variables were raised (compare equations 5.1 and 5.3). This is the theoretical basis of that method.

It suffers, however, from the defect of having to consider the worst possible case. It is common sense that in practice errors will rarely combine additively. Can we arrive at a more realistic estimate of their combination?

If n measurements of both x and y have been made, the sample variance of u is given by

$$s_u^2 = (1/n) \Sigma (u_i - \bar{u})^2$$

$$= (1/n) \Sigma (\delta u)^2$$

Substituting for δu from equation 5.2 and multiplying out

$$s_u^2 = \frac{1}{n} \left\{ \Sigma \left(\frac{\partial u}{\partial x} \delta x \right)^2 + \Sigma \left(\frac{\partial u}{\partial y} \delta y \right)^2 + 2 \Sigma \frac{\partial u}{\partial x} \frac{\partial u}{\partial y} \delta x \delta y \right\}$$

Residuals of x or y are equally likely to be of either sign, and so may their products $\delta x \delta y$. For large values of n, therefore, there will be as many positive as there are negative products within the summation sign of the third term, hence the term itself will tend to zero. Rearranging

$$s_u^2 = \left(\frac{\partial u}{\partial x}\right)^2 \frac{\Sigma(\delta x)^2}{n} + \left(\frac{\partial u}{\partial y}\right)^2 \frac{\Sigma(\delta y)^2}{n}$$

$$= \left(\frac{\partial u}{\partial x}\right)^2 s_x^2 + \left(\frac{\partial u}{\partial y}\right)^2 s_y^2 \tag{5.4}$$

This result, like the previous one, can be extended to include any number of variables; that is, the resultant error in an expression containing j variables $v_1, v_2, \ldots v_j$, is

$$s_f^2 = \sum_{i=1}^{j} \left(\frac{\partial f}{\partial v_i}\right)^2 s_i^2 \tag{5.5}$$

Equation 5.5 is called the *Superposition of Errors Theorem,* and is a basic result to which we shall be referring frequently. Note that n no longer appears explicitly in equations 5.4 and 5.5, so that in fact the number of individual observations does not have to be the same for each variable.

Applying the theorem to equation 5.1

$$s_g^2 = \left(\frac{\partial g}{\partial L}\right)^2 s_L^2 + \left(\frac{\partial g}{\partial T}\right)^2 s_T^2$$

$$= \left(\frac{4\pi^2}{T^2}\right)^2 s_L^2 + \left(-\frac{8\pi^2 L}{T^3}\right)^2 s_T^2$$

$$= \left(\frac{4\pi^2 L}{T^2}\right)^2 \frac{s_L^2}{L^2} + \left(\frac{4\pi^2 L}{T^2}\right)^2 \frac{4s_T^2}{T^2}$$

Dividing across by g^2

$$\left(\frac{s_g}{g}\right)^2 = \left(\frac{s_L}{L}\right)^2 + \left(\frac{2s_T}{T}\right)^2 \tag{5.6}$$

If we compare this with equation 5.3 by setting $s_g \equiv \delta g$, etc. it can be seen that equation 5.6 will yield a numerically smaller result for the proportional error in the derived quantity. Note, however, that there are many complicated expressions which cannot be recast in the simple 'proportional error' form of equation 5.6.

An important application of the superposition of errors theorem is in experimental design. Inspection of equation 5.6, for instance, shows us that the proportional error in T will have twice as much effect on the derived error as the proportional error in L. In this particular case the difference is not important, as it is actually rather easier to time a pendulum than to measure its length. Consider, however, the flow $\dot{V}$ of liquid of viscosity η through a capillary of radius a and length L under a pressure difference p given by

$$\dot{V} = \frac{\pi a^4 p}{8L\eta} \tag{5.7}$$

Suppose we wished to make use of this phenomenon to measure the viscosity of the liquid.

Rearranging equation 5.7 and applying the superposition of errors theorem gives us finally

$$\left(\frac{s_\eta}{\eta}\right)^2 = \left(\frac{s_p}{p}\right)^2 + \left(\frac{s_L}{L}\right)^2 + \left(\frac{s_{\dot V}}{\dot V}\right)^2 + \left(\frac{4 s_a}{a}\right)^2$$

In other words, the fractional error in a contributes four times as much to the derived error in η as any of the other variables. As the radius of a capillary is in any case very small and very difficult to measure, we might justifiably conclude that this is not a suitable experiment for viscosity determination, although much used for this purpose.

5.2 Weighting

We are now in a position to tackle the problem of the effective mean and resultant error due to combining a number of samples of observations of the same variable. In general these samples will have different means and standard errors, and may also of course contain different numbers of observations. The practice is to assign the mean of each sample a *weight* w such that the mean of the combination of samples is given by

$$\bar{X} = \frac{w_a \bar{x}_a + w_b \bar{x}_b + w_c \bar{x}_c + \dots}{w_a + w_b + w_c + \dots} \tag{5.8}$$

The question now is how to arrive at an appropriate value of the coefficient w. Consider for simplicity two samples only with means $\bar{x}_a$, $\bar{x}_b$ and standard deviations s_a, s_b. By definition the mean of their combination

$$\bar{X} = \frac{w_a \bar{x}_a + w_b \bar{x}_b}{w_a + w_b}$$

$$= \frac{\bar{x}_a + w \bar{x}_b}{1 + w}$$

where $w = w_b / w_a$.

From the superposition of errors theorem, the resultant error

$$s^2 = \left(\frac{\partial \bar{X}}{\partial \bar{x}_a}\right)^2 s_a^2 + \left(\frac{\partial \bar{X}}{\partial \bar{x}_b}\right)^2 s_b^2$$

$$\frac{\partial \bar{X}}{\partial \bar{x}_a} = \frac{1}{1 + w}, \qquad \frac{\partial \bar{X}}{\partial \bar{x}_b} = \frac{w}{1 + w}$$

So that

$$s^2 = \frac{s_a^2 + w^2 s_b^2}{(1 + w)^2} \tag{5.9}$$

According to the *Principle of Least Squares*, the best value of the weighted mean is that for which the (weighted) sum of the squares of the residuals is a minimum, that is

$$w_a(\bar{x}_a - \bar{X})^2 + w_b(\bar{x}_b - \bar{X})^2 \text{ is a minimum}$$

We can find the appropriate value of w in the usual way by differentiating the expression with respect to w and equating the differential to zero. This will be easier if we remember that the sum of the squares of the residuals must be proportional to the variance; we can therefore write the condition as

$$\frac{\partial s^2}{\partial w} = 0$$

then from equation 5.9

$$\frac{\partial}{\partial w} \left\{ \frac{s_a^2 + w s_b^2}{(1 + w)^2} \right\} = 0$$

This comes out as

$$w \left(= \frac{w_b}{w_a} \right) = \frac{s_a^2}{s_b^2} \tag{5.10}$$

This result can, like the previous ones, be extended to any number of samples. It is thus appropriate to assign weights in inverse proportion to the sample variances.

As it stands this system of weighting does not appear to take account of the possibility of different sample sizes. However, a similar result can be obtained if the variance is replaced by the square of the standard error of the mean, in which case variation of the number of observations in a sample is allowed for.

For example, the two sets of results of table 3.1 were found to have variances of 23.157 and $0.0015688\,g^2$ respectively. The corresponding standard errors of the mean were 1.819 and $0.01497\,g$ respectively, and the respective weights would thus be 0.3022 and 4462; that is, set B carries 15 000 times the weight of set A. In the circumstances there would be very little point in taking the observations of set A into account.

Weighting is most often used in experimental situations where it is possible to make only a limited number of observations and where the experimental parameters cannot always be optimised or even controlled. In such situations it is necessary to 'make the most of a bad job', to squeeze the maximum amount of information out of sets of observations which have been made under conditions which may have altered for reasons outside the control of the experimenter. Practical examples might include a rare physical event, an eclipse of the sun for instance, or a series of difficult and expensive determinations of some fundamental physical constant such as the velocity of light. It is characteristic of this type of problem that the observations cannot be treated as if they were all from the same population (otherwise they could simply be combined into a single sample).

Consider, for instance, two sets of measurements of the separation of the piers of a suspension bridge, made with a tellurometer. If the sets are made on successive days measured variations may be quite different due to changes in ambient temperature, wind speed or traffic density. Suppose the means and standard errors of the two sets of data are $(485.31 \pm 0.07)\,$m and $(484.96 \pm 0.11)\,$m. From equation 5.8 the best estimate of the combined mean will be

$$\bar{X} = \frac{485.31/0.07^2 + 484.96/0.11^2}{1/0.07^2 + 1/0.11^2}$$

$$= 485.023\,\text{m}$$

The standard error of the combined estimate can be found by combining equations 5.9 and 5.10

$$1/s^2 = 1/s_a^2 + 1/s_b^2$$

$$= 1/0.07^2 + 1/0.11^2$$

$$s = 0.059\,\text{m}$$

So the best information we now have about the separation of the piers is that it is $(485.023 \pm 0.059)\,$m.

5.3   Significance testing

The discussion of the last section raises the question of how we decide whether two samples are drawn from the same population. In general two such samples will have different means and variances; how do we establish whether the differences are *significant,* that is, whether each sample belongs to a separate population? There are two important practical situations when this knowledge will be useful. One is when, as in the last section, we wish to know how observations from different samples should be treated: can they be combined into a single sample or should we weight the means? The second and more important situation is where we wish to establish whether a change in experimental conditions has changed the result.

A number of tests of significance have been devised of which perhaps the most widely used are Student's *t*-test and Fisher's *F*-test.

5.3.1   Student's t-test

The pseudonym 'Student' concealed the identity of W. S. Gosset, who worked for an Edwardian brewery. His employers forbade him to publish his statistical work under his own name in order to conceal from their competitors the advanced nature of their product testing. He defined a statistic t as the ratio of the difference of the means of two samples to the standard deviation of the difference of their means, that is

$$t = \frac{\bar{x}_a - \bar{x}_b}{\sigma_{\bar{x}_a - \bar{x}_b}} \qquad\qquad (5.11)$$

As will shortly be shown, the denominator of equation 5.11 increases with sample variance. The statistic can therefore be thought of intuitively as a kind of figure of merit: for low t (small difference in means, large sample variance) the samples probably are from the same population; for high t (large difference in means, small sample variance) the samples are probably from different populations (figure 5.1). We will now try to put this on a more quantitative footing, starting by finding the variance of the distribution of means.

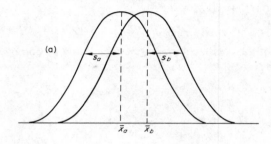

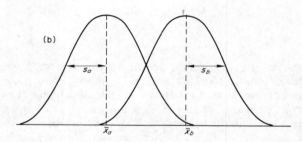

Figure 5.1. Two 'distributions' representing samples of nine observations each; $s_a = s_b = s$. (a) $\bar{x}_a - \bar{x}_b < 0.85s$: difference not significant at 10 per cent level. (b) $\bar{x}_a - \bar{x}_b > 2s$: difference significant at 0.1 per cent level.

Let us call Δ the difference of the two means, that is

$$\Delta = \bar{x}_a - \bar{x}_b \qquad (5.12)$$

Then equation 5.11 becomes

$$t = \Delta/\sigma_\Delta \qquad (5.13)$$

Applying the superposition of errors theorem to equation 5.12

$$\sigma_\Delta^2 = \left(\frac{\partial \Delta}{\partial \bar{x}_a}\right)^2 \sigma_{\bar{x}_a}^2 + \left(\frac{\partial \Delta}{\partial \bar{x}_b}\right)^2 \sigma_{\bar{x}_b}^2$$

Both differentials are unity, hence

$$\sigma_\Delta^2 = \sigma_{\bar{x}_a}^2 + \sigma_{\bar{x}_b}^2$$

If we assume that the two samples *are* from the same population, then from chapter 4

$$\sigma_{\bar{x}_a}^2 = \sigma^2/n_a, \ \sigma_{\bar{x}_b}^2 = \sigma^2/n_b$$

Hence

$$\sigma_\Delta^2 = \sigma^2(1/n_a + 1/n_b)$$
$$= \sigma^2(n_a + n_b)/n_a n_b \tag{5.14}$$

It only remains to express the population variance in terms of the sample variances. We remember that sample and population variances are related by Bessel's correction

$$\sigma^2 = n_a s_a^2/(n_a - 1)$$

or

$$n_a s_a^2 = (n_a - 1)\,\sigma^2$$

Similarly

$$n_b s_b^2 = (n_b - 1)\,\sigma^2$$

Adding

$$n_a s_a^2 + n_b s_b^2 = (n_a + n_b - 2)\,\sigma^2$$

or

$$\sigma^2 = \frac{n_a s_a^2 + n_b s_b^2}{n_a + n_b - 2}$$

Substituting back in equation 5.14

$$\sigma_\Delta^2 = \left(\frac{n_a s_a^2 + n_b s_b^2}{n_a + n_b - 2}\right)\left(\frac{n_a + n_b}{n_a n_b}\right)$$

So finally from equation 5.11

$$t = (\bar{x}_a - \bar{x}_b)\left[\left(\frac{n_a n_b}{n_a + n_b}\right)\left(\frac{n_a + n_b - 2}{n_a s_a^2 + n_b s_b^2}\right)\right]^{1/2} \tag{5.15}$$

$$= (\bar{x}_a - \bar{x}_b)\left[\left(\frac{n_a n_b}{n_a + n_b}\right)\left(\frac{\nu}{n_a s_a^2 + n_b s_b^2}\right)\right]^{1/2}$$

where $\nu = n_a + n_b - 2$ is the *number of degrees of freedom*.

The statistic t has its own family of probability distributions, one for every value of ν. The distributions are symmetrical and for large ν they tend to the form of the normal distribution (figure 5.2a). The area under any one of these curves between $\pm t$ is the probability that a pair of samples drawn from the same population will have a value of t within those limits; the area in the remaining tails (figure 5.2b) is the probability that the samples will have a value of t outside the limits.

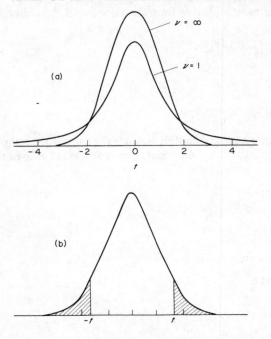

Figure 5.2. (a) Two curves of the family of *t*-distributions. (b) Typical *t*-curve. Total shaded area is the probability that this value will be exceeded by chance.

In practice values of *t* are computed corresponding to certain set areas of the tails, that is, to set probabilities that the value of *t* will lie outside the quoted limits. Sets of these values have been calculated for a range of values of ν (appendix A). Thus for $\nu = 5$, 10 per cent of all pairs of samples will have numerical values of *t* greater than 2·02; 1 per cent will have $|t| \geqslant 4.03$ and 0.1 per cent will have $|t| \geqslant 6.9$. This means that if we calculate for a given pair of samples $\nu = 5$, $|t| = 2.5$, there is less than one chance in ten that both samples came from the same population; if $|t| = 8$, the chance is less than one in a thousand. In the first case we would say that their difference was *significant at the 10 per cent level* but not at the 5 per cent level; in the second case that their difference was significant at the 0.1 per cent level.

It is important to bear in mind that these are *arbitrary* criteria. They have more in common with the standard of proof required by juries than with that required by mathematicians. Clearly a difference which could only arise once in a thousand experiments by chance is more impressive than one which could arise once in ten. How much more impressive one finds this difference is a subjective matter. As a rule of thumb a level of significance of 1 per cent is accepted by the majority of experimenters as evidence of a real difference. For a crucial experiment a level of significance of 0.1 per cent or even higher might be more appropriate, just as a jury might reasonably demand a higher standard of proof in a hanging matter. No purely statistical criterion can give us absolute certainty, but it can give us a very accurate balance of probabilities; and many men have been justly hanged on flimsier evidence.

Let us now apply our test to the example of the last section. Suppose the two sets of measurements contained five and seven observations respectively. Then we have

$$\bar{x}_a = 485.31 \text{ m}, \quad n_a = 5, \quad s_a^2 = 0.0156 \text{ m}^2$$
$$\bar{x}_b = 484.96 \text{ m}, \quad n_b = 7, \quad s_b^2 = 0.0622 \text{ m}^2$$

Substituting these values in equation 5.15

$$t = (485.31 - 484.96) \left[\frac{(5 \times 7)(5 + 7 - 2)}{(5 + 7)(5 \times 0.0156 + 7 \times 0.0622)} \right]^{1/2}$$

$$= 2.64$$

with $5 + 7 - 2 = 10$ degrees of freedom.

Entering the tables for $\nu = 10$, we find $t = 2.23$ at the 5 per cent level and 2.76 at the 2 per cent level. The difference between the two sets of readings is therefore significant at the 5 per cent level but not at the 2 per cent level. On the basis of this result there would be some justification for combining the observations directly; however, the prudent course would be to treat them as we did, as if they came from different populations.

5.3.2   Variance ratio or F-test

There are occasions when we need a method of comparison of two samples which does not involve the difference of their means. Consider, for instance, the fluctuations of transmission-line voltages about their mean level as demand alters. The mean here is arbitrary (and is probably constrained to be constant) and we are interested only in the variations, say between one day and another. Consider again a lathe whose setting is altered. The magnitude of the alteration is arbitrary; we are interested only in changes in the precision of manufacture, that is, whether the degree of variation in manufactured components has altered. In both these cases the t-test is inapplicable, as we do not have a difference of means to work with, and we must use *Fisher's F-test*.

The statistic F is defined as the ratio of the *best estimates* of the population variances given by each of the two samples

$$F = \sigma_a^2 / \sigma_b^2$$

These can be related to the variances of the samples themselves by Bessel's correction

$$F = \left(\frac{n_a}{n_a - 1} \right) s_a^2 \left/ \left(\frac{n_b}{n_b - 1} \right) s_b^2 \right. \tag{5.16}$$

The number of degrees of freedom of the two samples are

$$\nu_a = n_a - 1, \quad \nu_b = n_b - 1$$

There is an F-distribution, or rather a family of distributions, one for each pair of values of ν_a and ν_b (figure 5.3). The F-distributions, however, look rather different from the t-distributions. They are not symmetric but are skewed about their mode which is non-zero. A moment's thought will explain the phenomenon of the finite mode: unlike t, F must always be positive as it is a ratio of variances. As in the t-distribution, the area under the distribution curve between arbitrary values of F is the probability that a given value of F will lie between those limits if the samples are from the same population.

Because of the asymmetry of the distributions, it is conventional to consider only values of $F > 1$, that is, to so arrange the ratio of variances that the greater is always the numerator. Then it is necessary to consider only the right-hand tail of the distribution (figure 5.3). Tables have been prepared of values of F (for various combinations of degrees of freedom) the probability of exceeding which is 5 per cent or 1 per cent. If the calculated value of F is larger than the value tabulated for, say, 1 per cent, the inference is that a ratio of variances of this magnitude would occur in less than one pair of samples in a hundred pairs drawn from the same population; that is, the ratio is significant at the 1 per cent level.

Consider the example of the last section, with

$$s_b^2 = 0.0622\,\text{m}^2, \quad n_b = 7, \quad s_a^2 = 0.0156\,\text{m}^2, \quad n_a = 5$$

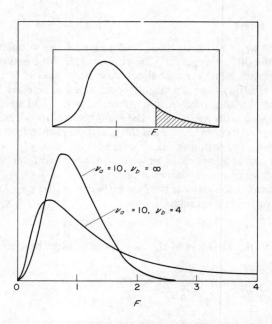

Figure 5.3. Two curves of the family of F-distributions (inset) shaded area is the probability that this value of F will be exceeded by chance.

From equation 5.16

$$F = \frac{5/4 \times 0.0156}{7/6 \times 0.0622}$$

$$= 0.268$$

$(\nu_a = 4, \ \nu_b = 6)$.

This is less than unity, so we interchange the suffixes a and b and obtain its reciprocal

$$F = 3.74, \quad \nu_a = 6, \quad \nu_b = 4$$

Entering the tables for $\nu_a = 6$ and $\nu_b = 4$, we find the 1 per cent limit given as 15.21 and the 5 per cent limit as 6.16. We therefore conclude that the difference in the two samples, as shown by the ratio of their variances, is not significant even at the 5 per cent level, that is, there is no good reason to suppose that they come from different populations.

6

Graphical Presentation

Graphical methods are unexcelled as a means of presenting the maximum amount of information in a concise and intelligible manner.

They are of particular value when exploring the relationship between variables or groups of variables. The experimenter frequently seeks to discover a functional relationship between variables. It is clearly of some importance if a connection can be established which is conveniently described in the form of a mathematical expression. For example, if the dependence of the pressure of a constant volume of gas upon the absolute temperature is examined, we expect there to be a relationship between the variables which is described by the simple expression

$$P = CT$$

where P is the pressure, T the absolute temperature and C a constant. If pressure is plotted against temperature the experimental points lie on or near a straight line, the amount of deviation depending upon the precision of the instruments and the skill of the operator.

Unfortunately, variables do not always behave obligingly. Consider the dependence of the wear of motor-car tyres upon mileage. A controlled experiment would undoubtedly show that this increased with mileage. We would not expect to be able to conclude that all tyres having completed say 15 000 miles have some particular degree of wear. Clearly, wear results from the operation of a number of random factors such as road surface, driving technique, and so on. A situation of this kind can only be described in limited statistical terms. Alternatively, we might be faced with completely uncharted waters, where it is by no means clear if there is any genuine connection between the variables. Suppose we wish to explore the possible effect of differing amounts of oil-additive upon cylinder-bore wear. If the additive is a new untried product we would be satisfied to establish if there is any significant connection at all between the variables, let alone try to describe it by means of a functional law. In statistical terminology, we would be exploring the degree of *correlation*. All these types of relationship between variables are important to engineers and will be considered in turn.

6.1 Functional relationships

Readings taken in the laboratory are subject to inevitable precision errors, and a statistical treatment is necessary to establish the best curve with which to represent the results. The simplest and most amenable relationship is a linear one. In many cases, a non-linear law may be manipulated into straight-line form.

Before continuing, it is important to be clear that when dealing with a functional relationship, the true values of x and y are assumed to lie on the best line and *the departures of the readings from the line are due solely to experimental errors.* There is no question of dealing with populations of x and y.

6.1.1 Fitting the best line when all the error is in one variable

In general, if we take experimental readings of the two variables x and y, both will be subject to precision errors. It will simplify matters if we let x be the controlled or independent variable which is assumed to be known exactly, while the dependent variable y, is subject to random errors of measurement. The case is not infrequently met in practice.

The line which best represents the dependence of y on x is defined as that which makes the sum of the squares of the distances from the experimental points to the line, measured in the direction of y, a minimum.

Let this line be

$$y = a + bx \tag{6.1}$$

and the rth pair of coordinates be x_r, y_r. Then for each point

$$y_r - a - bx_r = R_r$$

where R_r is the residual.

Our definition of the best line is that which makes $\Sigma (R_r)^2$ a minimum. For convenience, in the rest of this chapter, the sigma summation sign will be replaced by square brackets, thus

$$\Sigma (R_r)^2 \text{ is written as } [R_r^2]$$

The condition requiring $[R_r^2]$ to be a minimum is satisfied by partially differentiating $[R_r^2]$, first with respect to a, and then with respect to b, and in both cases equating to zero.

$$\frac{\partial [R_r^2]}{\partial a} = [y_r] - na - b[x_r] = 0$$

and

$$\frac{\partial [R_r^2]}{\partial b} = [x_r y_r] - a[x_r] - b[x_r^2] = 0$$

Rewriting these, we have what are usually called the *Normal Equations* (from now on, we shall drop the suffix r, it being understood that x and y refer to experimental values)

$$[y] = na + b[x] \tag{6.2}$$

$$[xy] = a[x] + b[x^2] \tag{6.3}$$

If equation 6.2 is divided throughout by n, the number of pairs of points; then

$$\bar{y} = a + b\bar{x} \tag{6.4}$$

Evidently, the best line passes through the mean values of x and y. To calculate a and b, equations 6.2 and 6.3 are solved by Cramer's method, giving

$$\frac{a}{\begin{vmatrix} [y] & [x] \\ [xy] & [x^2] \end{vmatrix}} = \frac{b}{\begin{vmatrix} n & [y] \\ [x] & [xy] \end{vmatrix}} = \frac{1}{\begin{vmatrix} n & [x] \\ [x] & [x^2] \end{vmatrix}}$$

Hence

$$a = \frac{[y][x^2] - [x][xy]}{n[x^2] - [x]^2} \tag{6.5}$$

and

$$b = \frac{n[xy] - [x][y]}{n[x^2] - [x]^2} \tag{6.6}$$

A convenient alternative form of the denominator of a and b, is

$$n[x^2] - [x]^2 = n[(x - \bar{x})^2] \tag{6.7}$$

Also the numerator of b may be recast into the useful alternative forms, which are stated for future use

$$b\{n[x^2] - [x]^2\} = n[xy] - [x][y] \tag{6.8}$$

$$= n[(x - \bar{x})(y - \bar{y})] \tag{6.9}$$

$$= n[y(x - \bar{x})] \tag{6.10}$$

6.1.2   Precision of slope and intercept

It is necessary to assess the precision of the slope b, and the intercept a. We already have a measure in $[R_r^2]$, of the departure of the experimental values of y from the line. The *variance of y about the line* is given by

$$\sigma_y^2 = \frac{[R_r^2]}{n - 2}$$

where $(n - 2)$ is the number of degrees of freedom, since two restrictions have been imposed in calculating $\bar{y}$ and b.

6.1.3   Standard error of slope

The slope of the line b may be expressed as

$$b = \frac{[y(x - \bar{x})]}{[(x - \bar{x})^2]} \qquad (6.11)$$

by substituting 6.7 and 6.10 into 6.6.

Expanding this

$$b = (1/[(x - \bar{x})^2])\{y_1(x_1 - \bar{x}) + y_2(x_2 - \bar{x}) + \ldots + y_n(x_n - \bar{x})\}$$

Here $y_1, y_2, \ldots y_n$ are independently observed values of y and in this context the terms in x are regarded as constants. Hence

$$b = k_1 y_1 + k_2 y_2 + \ldots + k_n y_n$$

where $k_1, k_2, \ldots k_n$ are the constants in x.

From the two propositions

(a) The variance of the sum of a number of independent events is the sum of the variances.

(b) The variance of ay is equal to a^2 (variance of y), it follows that

$$\text{Variance of } b = \frac{[(x - \bar{x})^2]}{[(x - \bar{x})^2]^2} \; \text{Variance } (y)$$

$$\sigma_b^2 = \frac{\sigma_y^2}{[(x - \bar{x})^2]}$$

and the standard error of b is given by

$$\text{s.e.}_b = \frac{\sigma_y}{[(x - \bar{x})^2]^{1/2}} \qquad (6.12)$$

6.1.4 Standard error of the intercept

The variance of the intercept a, is found simply from

$$\text{Variance } (a) = \text{Variance } (\bar{y} - b\bar{x})$$

$\bar{x}$, the mean value of x, is treated as a constant; hence

$$\text{Variance } (a) = \text{Variance } (\bar{y}) + (\bar{x})^2 \; \text{Variance } (b)$$

The variance of $\bar{y}$ is known to be given by

$$\text{Variance } (\bar{y}) = \frac{\text{Variance } (y)}{n} = \frac{\sigma_y^2}{n}$$

and the variance of b is

$$\frac{\sigma_y^2}{[(x - \bar{x})^2]}$$

so that

$$\text{Variance } a = \frac{\sigma_y^2}{n} + (\bar{x})^2 \; \frac{\sigma_y^2}{[(x - \bar{x})^2]}$$

which may be simplified to

$$\sigma_a^2 = \frac{\sigma_y^2 [x^2]}{n [(x - \bar{x})^2]}$$

Hence the standard error of a is

$$\text{s.e.}_a = \sigma_y \left(\frac{[x^2]}{n [(x - \bar{x})^2]} \right)^{1/2} \tag{6.13}$$

Before leaving the linear case we draw attention to a systematic way of presenting the relationship between the coefficients of the Normal Equations and the variances of a and b. Rewriting the Normal Equations 6.2 and 6.3 remembering that a and b are the unknowns

$$[y] = na + [x]b$$
$$[xy] = [x]a + [x^2]b$$

The results of the previous analysis may be concisely presented as follows

$$\frac{\sigma_a^2}{[x^2]} = \frac{\sigma_b^2}{n} = \frac{\sigma_y^2}{\begin{vmatrix} n & [x] \\ [x] & [x^2] \end{vmatrix}}$$

The denominator of σ_y^2 is the determinant formed from the coefficients of the right-hand side of the Normal Equations. The denominators of σ_a^2 and σ_b^2 are the minors, formed by taking the terms on the diagonal of the coefficient determinant in turn, that is, the minor of n is $[x^2]$, which is the denominator of σ_a^2, and the minor of $[x^2]$ is n, the denominator of σ_b^2. The procedure for fitting a best straight line is illustrated by means of an example.

Example 6.1

To examine the functional relationship between the fuel-consumption and power output for an oil-engine running at constant speed.

It is not necessary to concern ourselves with the details of the experiment, except to note that the power was measured with greater precision than the fuel consumption.

From experience, a linear relationship is expected over the range of the results. Readers mature enough to remember the days of steam-engines or who have an historical interest in steam will recall that the relationship between consumption and power was known as the Willan's line. The name is still occasionally applied to other types of engine.

A word of caution is necessary; it would be out of order to extrapolate the line beyond the experimental results. In this particular case, at higher powers the thermal efficiency of the engine decreases and the fuel-consumption line begins to turn upwards with an increasing slope and the equation would no longer apply. The experimental results are set out in table 6.1.

As we are assuming the errors to lie in the measurements of fuel consumption, we minimise the residuals in y.

Table 6.1. Experimental values of fuel consumption and power output for a single-cylinder oil-engine running at constant speed

Output (x) kW	Fuel consumption (y) kg/h
4.0	2.6
4.1	2.0
5.5	4.0
8.0	4.0
9.0	4.1
10.0	6.5
12.0	7.2
15.0	7.0
16.5	7.6
17.0	8.8
19.5	8.9
21.0	10.4
24.0	10.6
25.0	12.2

The mean values of x and y are

$$\bar{x} = 13.6143$$

$$\bar{y} = 6.8500$$

and the number of pairs of results is 14. From equation 6.11

$$b = \frac{[y(x - \bar{x})]}{[(x - \bar{x})^2]}$$

$$= \frac{286.6403}{665.6766} = 0.4306$$

The slope of the best line is 0.4306. As the line passes through the point $\bar{x}, \bar{y}$, the intercept is calculated directly from equation 6.4

$$a = \bar{y} - b\bar{x}$$

$$= 6.85 - (0.4306 \times 13.6142)$$

Hence, the intercept

$$a = 0.9877$$

To calculate the variance of y about the line we will anticipate a result derived later (equation 6.22)

$$[R_r^2] = [(y_r - \bar{y})^2] - b^2[(x - \bar{x})^2]$$

$$= 129.5014 - 0.1854 \times 665.6766$$

$$= 6.085$$

and

$$\sigma_y^2 = \frac{[R_r^2]}{n-2}$$

$$= \frac{6.085}{14-2}$$

$$= 0.5071$$

and therefore

$$\sigma_y = 0.7121$$

The standard error of the slope is given by equation 6.12

$$\text{s.e.}_b = \frac{\sigma_y}{[(x-\bar{x})^2]^{1/2}}$$

$$= \frac{0.7121}{(665.6766)^{1/2}}$$

$$= 0.0276$$

and from equation 6.13 the standard error of the intercept is

$$\text{s.e.}_a = \sigma_y \left(\frac{[x^2]}{n[(x-\bar{x})^2]} \right)^{1/2}$$

$$= 0.7121 \left(\frac{3250.55}{14 \times 665.6766} \right)^{1/2} = 0.4213$$

The functional relationship between fuel consumption y in kg/h and output x in kW for this engine, over the range spanned by the results, may be expressed as

$$y = (0.431 \pm 0.028)x + 0.99 \pm 0.42$$

where the limits of the slope and intercept are standard errors. It is important to state how the errors have been calculated. Some writers use other limits; for instance, the probable error, and confusion may, and often does, arise. A plot of the results and the best line are shown in figure 6.1.

6.1.5 Fitting the best curve

If the experimental points do not suggest that the variables are linearly related, it may be that a polynomial is better suited as a representative law.
Let

$$y = a + bx + cx^2 + \ldots$$

Applying the same principle as for the previous linear case, we minimise $[R_r^2]$ by differentiating with respect to a, b and c and equating to zero. Three normal equations result, which if compared with 6.2 and 6.3 will reveal a clear pattern.

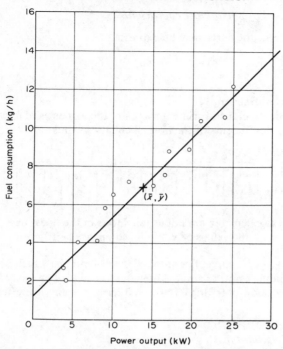

Figure 6.1. The best line representing fuel consumption against output for an oil-engine running at constant speed. All the errors are assumed to be in the measurements of fuel consumption.

$$[y] = na + b[x] + c[x^2]$$
$$[xy] = a[x] + b[x^2] + c[x^3]$$
$$[x^2y] = a[x^2] + b[x^3] + c[x^4]$$

These again may be solved by Cramer's method. Rarely are high polynomials required, but if a computer is employed, their solution presents no basic difficulty. As the number of terms get larger, one of the iterative methods, such as that by Gauss and Seidl, or an elimination method may be found to give a more economic solution.

The solution of the Normal Equation for a parabola, by Cramer's method, is

$$\cfrac{a}{\begin{vmatrix} [y] & [x] & [x^2] \\ [xy] & [x^2] & [x^3] \\ [x^2y] & [x^3] & [x^4] \end{vmatrix}} = \cfrac{b}{\begin{vmatrix} [n] & [y] & [x^2] \\ [x] & [xy] & [x^3] \\ [x^4] & [x^2y] & [x^4] \end{vmatrix}}$$

$$= \cfrac{c}{\begin{vmatrix} n & [x] & [y] \\ [x] & [x^2] & [xy] \\ [x^2] & [x^3] & [x^2y] \end{vmatrix}} = \cfrac{1}{\begin{vmatrix} n & [x] & [x^2] \\ [x] & [x^2] & [x^3] \\ [x^2] & [x^3] & [x^4] \end{vmatrix}}$$

6.1.6   *Standard errors of polynomial coefficients*

The variance of y about the curve may be expressed as

$$\sigma_y^2 = \frac{[R_r]^2}{n-3}$$

with $(n-3)$ degrees of freedom.

Following the rule developed for the linear case, the variances of a, b and c are derived from the coefficients of the normal equations thus

$$\frac{\sigma_a^2}{\begin{vmatrix} [x^2] & [x^3] \\ [x^3] & [x^4] \end{vmatrix}} = \frac{\sigma_b^2}{\begin{vmatrix} n & [x^2] \\ [x^2] & [x^4] \end{vmatrix}} = \frac{\sigma_c^2}{\begin{vmatrix} n & [x] \\ [x] & [x^2] \end{vmatrix}} = \frac{\sigma_y^2}{\begin{vmatrix} n & [x] & [x^2] \\ [x] & [x^2] & [x^3] \\ [x^2] & [x^3] & [x^4] \end{vmatrix}}$$

The standard errors so calculated are not as reliable as in the linear case. Difficulties arise because the values of x, x^2 and so on, are clearly not independent.

Also, when fitting a best curve, the order of the polynomial which best fits the experimental points is not, as a rule, known beforehand. Tests may be required to see if the addition of higher powered terms has any real effect upon the fit.

6.1.7   *Non-linear relationships*

Suppose that a case arises where the physics of the problem suggests a non-linear law is appropriate and we wish to fit a curve of the form

$$y = A\,e^{Bx} \tag{6.14}$$

Differentiation of $(y - A^{Bx})^2$ is not helpful and we are in some difficulty.
We may, of course, take logs and write

$$\ln y = \ln A + Bx$$

and obtain a straight line in plotting $\ln y$ against x. However, this is not really in the spirit of our method of dealing with errors, as y is the measured quantity, not $\ln y$. However, we may approach the problem by minimising the value of

$$[w_r(\ln y_r - \ln A - Bx_r)^2]$$

where w_r is an appropriate weighting.
We know from chapter 5 that such a weighting should be inversely proportional to the square of the residual.
Let $Y_r = \ln y_r$, then

$$s(Y_r)^2 = \frac{\delta(y_r)^2}{y_r^2}$$

therefore

$$w_r \propto \frac{1}{s(Y_r)^2} \propto y_r^2$$

If we assume an equal liability to error for all observations we must minimise

$$[y_r^2(\ln y_r - \ln A - Bx_r)^2]$$

The Normal Equations now become

$$[y_r^2 \ln y] = [y_r^2] \ln A + [x_r y_r^2] B$$

$$[xy^2 \ln y] = [x_r y_r^2] \ln A + [x_r^2 y_r^2] B$$

Hence the values of A and B are obtained in the usual way from the solution of these equations.

6.2   Linear regression and correlation

We turn now to methods of investigating and describing the relationship between variables which, though not functionally related, may to some degree have an influence upon each other.

Consider two variables x and y, for which the pairs of values have been plotted in the usual way, with y as ordinates and x as abscissa. In general the points will be scattered over the page and a trend may or may not be apparent.

The analysis is commenced by drawing a line using the experimental values of x, and minimising the sum of the squares of the residuals in y. This process gives the *regression line of y on x*. The arithmetic involved is exactly as that used when fitting the best line, assuming all the error to be in the values of y.

The Normal Equations are formed and a and b calculated as before; however, an alternative notation is favoured. By substituting equations 6.7 and 6.9 into 6.6

$$b = \frac{[(x - \bar{x})(y - \bar{y})]}{[(x - \bar{x})^2]} \tag{6.16}$$

and dividing the numerator and denominator by $(n - 1)$ we have

$$b = \frac{[(x - \bar{x})(y - \bar{y})]}{(n - 1)\sigma_x^2}$$

The expression

$$\frac{[(x - \bar{x})(y - \bar{y})]}{n - 1} \tag{6.17}$$

is called the *covariance* of x and y.

Hence

$$b = \frac{\text{covariance }(xy)}{\text{variance }(x)}$$

and b is the *regression coefficient of y on x*.

The line passes through $\bar{x}$, $\bar{y}$, and hence its equation is

$$y - \bar{y} = \frac{\text{covariance }(xy)}{\text{variance }(x)}(x - \bar{x}) \tag{6.18}$$

A second line may be drawn, this time taking the values of y as exact, and minimising the sum of the square of the residuals in x. The equation of this, the *regression line of x and y,* will be

$$x - \bar{x} = \frac{\text{covariance } (xy)}{\text{variance } y} (y - \bar{y}) \tag{6.19}$$

We now have two lines, each derived in a different way, and both passing through $\bar{x}, \bar{y}$. Equations 6.18 and 6.19 are unusual in the mathematical sense in that there is no algebraic connection between them. If the origin is moved to $\bar{x}, \bar{y}$ and the scales changed by letting

$$Y = y/\sigma_y \qquad X = x/\sigma_x$$

then the equations 6.18 and 6.19 for the regression lines transform to, for y on x

$$Y = \frac{\text{covariance } (xy)}{\sigma_x \sigma_y} X$$

and for x on y

$$X = \frac{\text{covariance } (xy)}{\sigma_x \sigma_y} Y$$

The factor

$$\frac{\text{covariance } (xy)}{\sigma_x \sigma_y}$$

is called the *correlation coefficient r* and its value may vary from +1 to −1. As its name suggests, it provides a measure of the interrelationship between the variables. When y increases as x increases, y and x are said to be positively correlated. If on the other hand the correlation coefficient is negative, y and x are negatively correlated. When the lines coincide the angles θ in figure 6.2 are $45°$ and the correlation coefficient is +1; this means that there is no scatter of the experimental points. The greater the scatter of the experimental points, the smaller the correlation coefficient and the less confident are we about the interdependence of the variables.

The point was made earlier that when dealing with a functional relationship we are concerned only with the experimental values of x and y and the errors. When drawing the regression lines and studying the correlation we are considering the populations of values of x and y. The regression of y on x refers to the population of y for a given value of x, and the regression of x on y refers to the population of x for a given value of y.

We shall return to discuss the significance of the correlation coefficient later.

6.2.1   Analysis of variance

Let us now take a second look at the problem of describing the scatter of experimental points. For each value of x there is a point y on the regression line

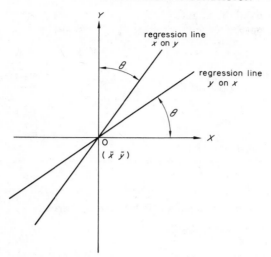

Figure 6.2. Regression lines of y on x and x on y for the same set of measurements, referred to an origin $\bar{x}, \bar{y}$ to show the identity of the correlation coefficients.

corresponding to the experimental value y_r. For a single reading

$$y_r - y = (y_r - \bar{y}) - (y - \bar{y})$$

It is not difficult to show that, for all the values

$$[(y_r - y)^2] = [(y_r - \bar{y})^2] - [(y - \bar{y})^2] \qquad (6.21)$$

That is, the sum of the squares about the regression line is equal to the sum of the squares about the mean, less the sum of the squares due to regression about the mean.

The first term is recognised as the sum of the squares of the residuals $[R_r^2]$. As the equation of the line is

$$y - \bar{y} = b(x - \bar{x})$$

then

$$[(y - \bar{y})^2] = b^2 [(x - \bar{x})^2]$$

Equation 6.21 may now be written

$$[R_r^2] = [(y_r - \bar{y})^2] - b^2[(x - \bar{x})^2] \qquad (6.22)$$

We see that it is not necessary to calculate $[R_r^2]$ directly, it may be found as the difference of the readily available terms on the right-hand side of the equation 6.22 (table 6.2).

The value obtained is referred to the F-tables with the appropriate degrees of freedom, that is, 1 and $(n - 2)$ respectively, and hence the probability of the distribution of the results occurring by chance is obtained.

Alternatively, the problem may be approached in a somewhat different manner, by examining the regression coefficient.

Table 6.2. Analysis of variance

Description	Sum of squares	Degrees of freedom	Mean squares
Due to regression	$[(y - \bar{y})^2]$ $= b^2[(x - \bar{x})^2]$	1	$\dfrac{b^2[(x - \bar{x})^2]}{1}$
About regression	$[(y_r - y)^2]$ $= [R_r^2]$	$n - 2$	$\dfrac{[R_r^2]}{n - 2} = \sigma_{\bar{y}}^2$
Total	$[(y_r - \bar{y}^2)]$	$n - 1$	

6.2.2 *Standard error of the regression coefficient and the intercept*

The standard errors of b and a are found in a similar manner to that used when deriving the best straight line.

$$\text{s.e.}_b = \frac{\sigma_y}{[(x - \bar{x})^2]^{1/2}} \tag{6.24}$$

where

$$\sigma_y^2 = [R_r^2]/(n - 2)$$

and

$$\text{s.e.}_a = \sigma_y \left(\frac{[x^2]}{n[(x - \bar{x})^2]} \right)^{1/2} \tag{6.25}$$

If there is no certain correlation between the variables, the regression coefficient b, for the regression of y on x, would be zero. We may use the t-test to see if b is significantly different from zero.

Calculating t from

$$t = |b|/\text{s.e.}_b \tag{6.26}$$

we refer to the tables to find the probability of the calculated value of t occurring by chance. The tables are entered for $(n - 2)$ degrees of freedom.

The two tests, using F and t, are really equivalent and the numerical value of F is equal to t^2.

A useful and easy statistic to calculate is the percentage fit, which gives some indication of the quality of the relationship between the variables.

$$\text{Percentage fit} = \frac{100 \times \text{sum of squares due to regression}}{\text{total sum of squares}}$$

$$= \frac{100 \times b^2[(x - \bar{x})^2]}{[(y_r - \bar{y})^2]}$$

Another obvious way of testing the results is to compare the overall range of the variables with the magnitude of the scatter about the regression line. The greater the ratio of the former to the latter, the more inclined shall we be to accept the regression relationship as valid.

To test if the mean square due to regression is significantly greater than the mean square about the regression line, calculate F, where

$$F = \frac{\text{mean square due to regression}}{\text{mean square about regression line}}$$

$$= \frac{b^2[(x - \bar{x})^2]}{\sigma_y^2} \tag{6.23}$$

6.2.3 Significance of the correlation coefficient

It has already been said that the regression is concerned with populations of values, hence r is an estimate of ρ, the correlation coefficient for the population.

To test the significance of r we use the hypothesis that the value of r obtained for a set of results could, at some chosen level of probability, be from a normal population whose value of ρ is zero. If this were so, the variables would, of course, be uncorrelated.

To do this we need the distribution of r for ρ equals zero. It has been seen that F is related to t and it is clear that both must be related to r. It may be shown that

$$t = r\left(\frac{n-2}{1-r^2}\right)^{1/2} \tag{6.27}$$

Hence, t is calculated and the t-tables entered at an appropriate level of probability for $(n - 2)$ degrees of freedom.

Alternatively, a modified table is provided at the back of the book which lists r for a range of probabilities and degrees of freedom. Again the table is entered at $(n - 2)$ degrees of freedom.

Finally, if it is found that the regression is significant, claims must be made with caution and restricted to within the boundaries of the investigation. It does not follow that a 'cause and effect' has been discovered; some unconsidered variable may be responsible for the variation.

Also, if the linear regression is poor it does not necessarily mean that the variables are uncorrelated. A parabola or polynomial may fit the data very well and a curvilinear regression reveal a high degree of correlation. Curvilinear regression is performed by fitting the best curve, as described earlier in this chapter. The analysis of the variance and assessment of the standard errors follows much the same lines as for the linear case. However, a detailed study of curvilinear regression is beyond the scope of this book. The procedure of fitting a regression line is illustrated by means of a worked example.

Example 6.2

Suppose we wish to investigate if there is any relationship between the 0.2 per cent extension yield-point and Young's modulus E for a number of commercially important alloys.

By performing a linear regression we shall see if there appears to be any interrelationship between these two very different physical characteristics of the alloys. The results of tests on sixteen different alloys are shown in table 6.3.

Table 6.3. Experimental values of yield-point and Young's modulus for a number of commercial alloys

Yield point (x) kN/mm^2	Young's modulus (y) kN/mm^2
0.167	20
0.045	47
0.234	67
0.333	133
0.400	100
0.567	120
0.630	260
0.630	200
0.700	153
0.800	213
1.000	246
1.000	286
1.030	196
1.230	207
1.330	267
1.470	200

We start the analysis by finding the slope and intercept of the regression line $(y$ on $x)$.

Firstly, the mean values of x and y are

$$\bar{x} = 0.7229$$

$$\bar{y} = 169.6875$$

The number of pairs of results is

$$n = 16$$

The slope or regression coefficient is found, as before, from equation 6.11

$$b = \frac{[y(x - \bar{x})]}{[(x - \bar{x})^2]}$$

$$= 151.533$$

As the line passes through the point $\bar{x}, \bar{y}$, the intercept is calculated directly using

$$a = \bar{y} - b\bar{x}$$

$$= 60.148$$

Hence the equation of the regression line for y on x, is

$$y = 151.533x + 60.148$$

To calculate the variance of y about the regression line, first find the sum of the squares of the residuals in y

$$[R_r^2] = [(y - \bar{y})^2] - b^2[(x - \bar{x})^2]$$
$$= 99729.1554 - 63000.4654$$
$$= 36728.6900$$

and as

$$\sigma_y^2 = [R_r^2]/(n - 2)$$
$$= 36728.6900/14$$
$$= 2623.4779$$

Hence

$$\sigma_y = 51.2199$$

The standard error of the slope, from equation 6.24, is

$$\text{s.e.}_b = \sigma_y/[(x - \bar{x})^2]^{1/2}$$
$$= 30.9224$$

and from equation 6.25 the standard error of the intercept

$$\text{s.e.}_a = \sigma_y \left(\frac{[x^2]}{n[(x - \bar{x})^2]}\right)^{1/2}$$
$$= 25.761$$

Before proceeding, we shall test to see if b, the regression coefficient, differs significantly from zero.

Calculating t from equation 6.26

$$t = |b|/\text{s.e.}_b$$
$$= 151.533/30.922$$
$$= 4.9$$

Entering the t-tables at 0.001 level for 14 degrees of freedom, gives $t = 4.140$. Hence the regression relationship is highly significant.

From equation 6.17 the covariance is

$$\frac{[(x - \bar{x})(y - \bar{y})]}{n - 1} = 27.7171$$

and the standard deviations of x and y are

$$\sigma_x = 0.4277$$
$$\sigma_y = 81.5391$$

From equation 6.20 the correlation coefficient r is

$$\frac{\text{Covariance } (xy)}{\sigma_x \sigma_y} = \frac{27.7171}{0.4277 \times 81.5391}$$

$$r = 0.79$$

This, of course, gives a measure of the quality of the relationship between the variables. Before discussing the significance of r we shall analyse the variance more thoroughly by drawing up a variance table.

First, we shall calculate the percentage fit by dividing the sum of the squares due to regression by the total sum of the squares.

$$\text{Percentage fit} = 100 \times \frac{63000.4654}{99729.1554}$$

$$= 63$$

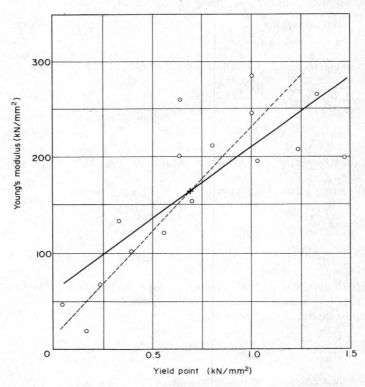

Figure 6.3. Regression lines of Young's modulus against yield-point for a number of commercially important alloys. The solid line is the regression line of Young's modulus on yield point, the broken line is the regression line of yield point on Young's modulus.

To test if the mean square due to regression is significantly greater than the mean square about the regression line, calculate F from

$$F = \frac{\text{Mean square due to regression}}{\text{Mean square about regression}}$$

$$= \frac{63000.4654}{2623.4779}$$

$$= 24$$

for 1 and 14 degrees of freedom. From the F-tables, we find that for probabilities of 0.05 and 0.01 the values of F are 4.60 and 8.86 respectively. Hence again it is shown that the regression is highly significant and the variates y and x are probably connected by a genuine relationship.

As mentioned previously, the F- and t-tests are related and numerically $F = 24$ is equal to $t^2 = 4.9^2$.

Finally, let us consider the significance of the correlation coefficient. Calculating t for $(n-2)$ degrees of freedom using equation 6.27

$$t = r \left(\frac{n-2}{1-r^2}\right)^{1/2} = 0.7948 \left(\frac{14}{1-0.7948^2}\right)^{1/2}$$

gives

$$t = 4.9$$

and as t at the 0.001 level, for 14 degrees of freedom, is 4.14, the correlation coefficient is highly significant.

For interest, we shall calculate the value of the regression coefficient b' for x (Young's modulus) on y (yield point).

$$b' = \frac{\text{covariance } (xy)}{\text{variance } (y)}$$

$$= \frac{27.7171}{6648.629} = 0.0042$$

The line is shown dotted in figure 6.3. It is clear that a significant correlation exists between E and the yield point.

The equation is of some importance to engineers as it indicates the capacity of a material to store elastic energy.

7

Dimensional Analysis

Dimensional analysis is a useful technique which can reduce what seems to be a very difficult and complex experimental situation to a much more straight-forward one. It is particularly helpful in problems where a rigorous theoretical analysis is difficult or impossible.

Consider the problem of predicting the heat transfer between two metal bars mated end-to-end in a vacuum. We can make a reasonable hypothesis about the variables involved; these will include the thermal conductivity of the metal, its surface hardness and roughness, and the force pressing the bars together. The theoretical analysis of the problem is very difficult. In engineering, however, we cannot choose our problems; any answer is better than none, and the answer to this particular problem has been required urgently at different times for the design of such diverse items as satellites and nuclear power stations.

One way of approaching the problem would be to conduct a series of heat transfer measurements while the load, say, was varied and all the other parameters were held constant. Then one other parameter, say the surface roughness, could be changed slightly and another series of heat transfer coefficients could be measured at various loads. This could be repeated a number of times, giving a family of curves of heat transfer versus load at different surface roughness. The whole series of experiments could then be gone through again with the surface roughness held constant and another parameter varied, giving another family of curves, and so on. Clearly this would need a very long and tedious experimental programme, and the results would not be particularly easy for a designer to interpret at a glance.

The application of dimensional analysis can simplify our experimental programme dramatically for the cost of a few minutes' work. The basis of the method is the so-called *principle of dimensional homogeneity,* which states that in any equation representing a physical relationship the dimensions of the left-hand side must be the same as the dimensions of the right-hand side. This is true for any system of dimensions we care to use. For instance, take the equation of motion

$$v = u + ft \tag{7.1}$$

v and u are the final and initial velocities which have the dimensions of length per unit time, f is an acceleration, with dimensions of velocity per unit time, and the time t, of course, has the dimensions of time. We write this conventionally as

$$[v] = [u] = LT^{-1}$$
$$[f] = LT^{-2}$$
$$[t] = T$$

Clearly

$$[ft] = LT^{-2}T$$
$$= LT^{-1} = [u] = [v]$$

and the dimensions of both sides of the equation are the same. (Note that we do not add the dimensions of the two terms on the right-hand side; we are only interested in the power to which each dimension is raised.) Note also that the dimensions of every term in the equation are the same.

These results are true whatever we do to the equation. Suppose we divide through by t

$$v/t = u/t + f$$
$$[v/t] = LT^{-1}T^{-1} = LT^{-2}$$
$$= [u/t] = [f] \qquad (7.2)$$

Again the dimensions of both sides, and the dimensions of each individual term, are the same. We would get the same result if we divided through by u or f.

If we divide through by u, however, we get a more interesting and useful result.

$$v/u = 1 + ft/u \qquad (7.3)$$

Now

$$[v/u] = LT^{-1}/LT^{-1} = 1$$
$$= [ft/u]$$

The dimensions cancel out and the groups v/u and ft/u are said to be *dimensionless*. For a given experimental situation, the numerical values of these dimensionless groups will be the same no matter what system of units they are measured in. If f is measured in miles per hour^2, u and v in miles per hour and t in hours, the numerical values of v/u and ft/u will be exactly the same as if f were in cm/s^2, v in cm/s and t in seconds.

Even more important, the equation has been reduced to a relationship between two variables. If we plot v/u against ft/u, we shall get a single unique curve which will represent the relationship between u, v, f and t for all four parameters. Dimensional analysis consists essentially of finding a set of dimensionless groups which will represent a physical relationship when the exact form of the relationship is not known beforehand.

We will consider a method for finding dimensionless groups first developed by Lord Rayleigh (J. W. Strutt, Third Baron Rayleigh).

7.1   Rayleigh's method

Rayleigh's method supposes that the unknown relationship may be written as a power series in the terms of products of the powers of the variables involved. Thus we would write

$$v = \phi(u^\alpha f^\beta t^\gamma) \tag{7.4}$$

which merely says that v is a function of the product in brackets where α, β, γ are unknown exponents. Now by the principle of dimensional homogeneity which we have just described, since

$$[v] = \phi[u^\alpha f^\beta t^\gamma]$$

then dimensionally

$$LT^{-1} = (LT^{-1})^\alpha (LT^{-2})^\beta T^\gamma$$
$$= L^{\alpha+\beta} T^{-\alpha-2\beta+\gamma}$$

For this relationship to be true, the exponent of each dimension on the left-hand side must be equal to the sum of the corresponding exponent on the right-hand side.

That is, for L

$$1 = \alpha + \beta \tag{i}$$

for T

$$-1 = -\alpha - 2\beta + \gamma \tag{ii}$$

Equations (i) and (ii) are called the *indicial equations*. Obviously there must be as many indicial equations as there are dimensions in the original problem. Note that we have three unknowns but only two equations; thus we cannot solve the equations explicitly. As we shall see, however, this does not matter.

Solving equations (i) and (ii) simultaneously for β, we obtain

$$\gamma = \beta$$
$$\alpha = 1 - \beta$$

Substituting in equation 7.4 gives

$$v = \phi(u^{1-\beta} f^\beta t^\beta)$$

Rearranging

$$v = u\phi(ft/u)^\beta$$

or

$$v/u = \phi(ft/u)^\beta \tag{7.5}$$

We have now obtained by dimensional analysis the two dimensionless groups. At first sight equation 7.5 appears to be quite different from equation 7.3. The functional form of equation 7.5 may be interpreted as the power series

$$v/u = C_0 + C_1(ft/u) + C_2(ft/u)^2 + \dots$$

But if $C_0 = C_1 = 1$ and $C_2 \ldots C_n = 0$ then we have

$$v/u = 1 + ft/u$$

which is equation 7.3.

Thus equation 7.5 is not a real equation at all, and the exponent has no physical significance whatsoever. This is very important to remember. Dimensional analysis will tell us which dimensionless groups take part in a physical relationship, but it cannot tell us the explicit form of the relationship. In this case, it will not tell us that $C_0 = C_1 = 1$ or that the rest of the coefficients are zero. This information may only be found, either from analysis where possible, or in complex cases where dimensional methods are useful, by experiment in the laboratory.

Now we are ready to return to our original problem. First we must choose a set of primary dimensions. These need not be restricted to mass, length and time; there is nothing inviolate about the dimensions of a particular variable and we may choose any consistent system we please. For heat-transfer problems it is often convenient to use quantity of heat Q and temperature θ as primary dimensions in addition to the usual three.

Thus the heat-transfer coefficient C is the quantity of heat which flows in unit time under a unit temperature difference, so

$$[C] = QT^{-1}\theta^{-1}$$

The thermal conductivity k is the quantity of heat which flows through a unit cube of the metal in unit time under unit temperature difference, so

$$[k] = QL^{-2}LT^{-1}\theta^{-1} = QL^{-1}T^{-1}\theta^{-1}$$

The surface hardness H is the pressure, that is, force per unit area, at which the surface starts to flow plastically

$$[H] = MLT^{-2}L^{-2} = ML^{-1}T^{-2}$$

The load W is simply a force

$$[W] = MLT^{-2}$$

and the surface roughness σ is a length

$$[\sigma] = L$$

We assume

$$C = k^\alpha H^\beta W^\gamma \sigma^\delta \tag{7.6}$$

then

$$[C] = [k^\alpha H^\beta W^\gamma \sigma^\delta]$$
$$QT^{-1}\theta^{-1} = (QL^{-1}T^{-1}\theta^{-1})^\alpha (ML^{-1}T^{-2})^\beta (MLT^{-2})^\gamma L^\delta$$
$$= Q^\alpha L^{-\alpha-\beta+\gamma+\delta} T^{-\alpha-2\beta-2\gamma} \theta^{-\alpha} M^{\beta+\gamma}$$

Equating indices

for Q $1 = \alpha$ (i)

for L $0 = -\alpha-\beta+\gamma+\delta$ (ii) for T $-1 = -\alpha - 2\beta - 2\gamma$ (iii)

for θ $-1 = -\alpha$ (iv)

for M $0 = \beta + \gamma$ (v)

Note that since L does not appear on the left-hand side we conclude that its exponent on that side must be zero. Note also that not all the indicial equations are independent; (i) and (iv) are equivalent and (iii) + (iv) is equivalent to (v). We shall return to this point later.

We thus again have one more unknown than the number of independent equations and cannot obtain an explicit solution. Solving the equations for β we obtain

$$\alpha = 1$$
$$\gamma = -\beta$$
$$\delta = 1 + 2\beta$$

Substituting back in equation 7.6

$$C = k^1 H^\beta W^{-\beta} \sigma^{1+2\beta}$$

or

$$\frac{C}{\sigma k} = \left(\frac{H\sigma^2}{W}\right)^\beta$$

Thus we have reduced a relation between five variables to a relation between two dimensionless groups; if we plot our experimental results as dimensionless conductance $C/\sigma k$ against dimensionless load $W/H\sigma^2$ we should obtain a single unique curve which will be true for any value of any of the five variables involved. Clearly this has simplified our experimental work enormously[5].

The fact that one parameter, σ, appears on each side of the equation is not a cause for alarm; this often happens and is quite in order.

Again the unknown exponent β has no physical significance. In this particular case the indicial equations admit of only one solution, but more usually the form of the dimensionless groups depend on the choice of exponent when the indicial equations are solved. Often several pairs of dimensionless groups could satisfy the criteria, and any of these pairs would be as correct as any other pair. In such a case it usually happens that one pair is more convenient to use than the others. If, for instance, the errors of measurements in one experimental parameter were much larger than in the others, it would not be convenient to choose a pair of dimensionless groups in which this parameter occurred in each group. Note that we chose five primary dimensions and obtained three independent indicial equations. This gave us $5 - 3 = 2$ dimensionless groups.

7.2 Buckingham's method

We will now examine a second and slightly different approach to the formation of dimensionless groups. This more systematic method uses the so-called Pi(π) theorem, first attributed to E. Buckingham. The theorem states that any homogeneous equation expressing a functional relationship between n variables, of the form

$$\phi(A, B, C, D \ldots) = 0$$

has a solution

$$\phi(\pi_1, \pi_2, \pi_3, \ldots \pi_{n-\nu}) = 0$$

where each π is a dimensionless group, n is the number of variables in the first equation and ν is the number of independent equations represented by the rows of the matrix (see later).

A mathematical justification for the π-theorem, and a demonstration that it is free from the confinement of the power series, exists but is outside the scope of this book.

In order to illustrate the use of the method consider two examples.

Example 1. Journal bearing

First, we will assume that we wish to investigate experimentally the torque due to friction in a journal bearing. The variables over which we have control are included in the equation

$$\phi(T, P, \eta, N, D) = 0$$

where

T = frictional torque
P = pressure/projected bearing area
η = viscosity of lubricant
N = rotational speed
D = bearing diameter

Let the fundamental units used be M, L and T.

The dimensional information is arranged in tabular form, where the indices of the fundamental units appear in the rows. Each column is numbered from the left-hand side K_1, K_2, K_3, etc.

	K_1	K_2	K_3	K_4	K_5
	T	P	η	N	D
M	1	1	1	0	0
L	2	−1	−1	0	1
T	−2	−2	−1	−1	0

The rank of the matrix formed by the indices is calculated. This is equal to the highest order of non-zero determinant which may be formed. In this case the rank is 3. The determinant formed from the last three columns gives

$$\begin{vmatrix} 1 & 0 & 0 \\ -1 & 0 & 1 \\ -1 & -1 & 0 \end{vmatrix} = -1$$

Returning to the interpretation to be placed on ν in the theorem, we may now state that ν is the rank of the dimensional matrix. In our case as $\nu = 3$, we expect to form $n - \nu = 5 - 3 = 2$ dimensionless groups.

In many cases, as in this, the rank of the matrix will be equal to the number of rows and therefore equal to the number of fundamental units. However, if the rank of the matrix is less than the number of rows, then this simply means that the dimensional equations are not independent and some may be disregarded.

Note also that the dimensional equation is arranged so that the determinant formed from the columns at the right-hand side of the matrix give a non-zero determinant of rank ν.

We now write the dimensional equation in terms of the Ks for each fundamental unit, in the following fashion

$$K_1 + K_2 + K_3 = 0 \qquad \text{(for M)}$$
$$2K_1 - K_2 - K_3 + K_5 = 0 \qquad \text{(for L)}$$
$$-2K_1 - 2K_2 - K_3 - K_4 = 0 \qquad \text{(for T)}$$

As two groups are expected and we would like T and P to appear independently, let us solve for K_3, K_4 and K_5 in terms of K_1 and K_2, that is the Ks which are associated with the variables T and P.

$$K_3 = -K_1 - K_2$$
$$K_4 = -K_1 - K_2 \qquad\qquad (7.7)$$
$$K_5 = -3K_1$$

Now let $K_1 = 1$ and $K_2 = 0$ in the above equation. Then

$$K_3 = -1$$
$$K_4 = -1$$
$$K_5 = 0$$

Similarly let $K_2 = 1$ and $K_1 = 0$ giving

$$K_3 = -1$$
$$K_4 = -1$$
$$K_5 = 0$$

We can now write out our dimensionless groups in matrix form using the values of the Ks just derived.

	K_1	K_2	K_3	K_4	K_5
	T	P	η	N	D
π_1	1	0	-1	-1	-3
π_2	0	1	-1	-1	0

Note in passing that the columns of equations 7.7 give the last three terms in the rows of the π matrix and could have been written immediately.

Collecting the terms from the matrix we have

$$\pi_1 = T/N\eta D^3$$
$$\pi_2 = P/N\eta$$

or

$$\phi(\pi_1, \pi_2) = 0$$
$$\phi(T/N\eta D^3, P/N\eta) = 0$$

Historically, the variables usually used have included F, the tangential force at the radius of the bearing $(D/2)$ and W, the load on the bearing. These could well have been taken as variables in the original assumptions, in place of T and P. However, as an exercise in manipulation we will change the groups obtained to the more familiar ones.

As T is proportional to FD (force × radius) and P is proportional to W/D^2 (force/area)

$$\frac{T}{N\eta D^3} \times \frac{N\eta}{P} = \frac{T}{PD^3}$$
$$= \frac{FD^3}{WD^3} = \frac{F}{W}$$

Hence the new groups are F/W and $P/N\eta$. $P/N\eta$ is the Sommerfeld number, named after an early worker in the field, and F/W is a coefficient of friction.

Now that we have established the method let us look at one further and perhaps more topical example.

Example 2. Elastohydrodynamic lubrication

The study of the lubrication of non-conforming surfaces involves both the elastic properties of the bodies and the viscosity of the lubricant. The extremely high pressure in the oil film at, nominally, line or point contact, has a profound effect upon the viscosity of the lubricant as it passes through the contact. This type of lubrication is referred to as *elastohydrodynamic.*

Considering the isothermal case, which is valid for situations where bodies are rolling together, the pressure–viscosity relationship usually assumed is

$$\eta = \eta_0 \exp(\alpha p)$$

where η_0 is the viscosity outside the contact and α is a constant having the same dimensions as $1/p$ and p is the pressure.

In seeking a dimensional relationship for film thickness h, we may select the following variables as relevant

h = film thickness
w = load per unit length
u = a surface velocity
α = viscosity coefficient
η = viscosity of lubricant
E' = elastic modulus of the materials
R = relative radius at the contact

We shall use the fundamental units M, L, T. Setting out the dimensions in tabular form we have

	K_1	K_2	K_3	K_4	K_5	K_6	K_7
	h	w	u	α	η	E'	R
M	0	1	0	-1	1	1	0
L	1	0	1	1	-1	-1	1
T	0	-2	-1	2	-1	-2	0

Here the rank of the matrix is 3, and the determinant on the right-hand side has a value, namely -1. Also the order of the variables has been selected to give groups containing h, w, u, and α independently.

We expect $7 - 3 = 4$ groups, then

$$K_2 - K_4 + K_5 + K_6 = 0$$
$$K_1 + K_3 + K_4 - K_5 - K_6 + K_7 = 0$$
$$-2K_2 - K_3 + 2K_4 - K_5 - 2K_6 = 0$$

Now solving for K_5, K_6, K_7 in terms of K_1, K_2, K_3 and K_4, we have

$$K_5 = K_3$$
$$K_6 = -K_2 - K_3 + K_4$$
$$K_7 = -K_1 - K_2 - K_3$$

Letting K_1, K_2, K_3, K_4 be unity in turn, while the remainder are zero we may now write down the groups immediately.

h	w	u	α	η	E'	R
1	0	0	0	0	0 0	-1
0	1	0	0	0	-1	-1
0	0	1	0	1	-1	-1
0	0	0	1	0	1	0

$\pi_1 = h/R$ a scale parameter or group

$\pi_2 = W/E'R$ a load parameter or group

$\pi_3 = u\eta/E'R$ a speed parameter or group

$\pi_4 = \alpha E'$ a materials parameter or group

Of course, many different groups may be formed. The ones selected here are similar to those used by Dowson and Higginson[6] in their solution of the elasto-hydrodynamic problem. Halling, according to Greenwood[7], prefers

$$h/R, \quad \eta u/W, \quad \alpha W/R \text{ and } E'R/W$$

here again each of these groups relates to a physical effect (vertical scale, hydrodynamic lift, viscosity variation and elasticity). Clearly the second set may be derived from the first. Other workers prefer other groups, but without discussing the mathematics of elastohydrodynamic lubrication, which is not our immediate purpose, we are not in a position to judge the merits of each case.

Situations very much more complex than the above can be and are treated successfully by dimensional analysis. In fluid dynamics, which contains many problems not susceptible to a rigorous approach, dimensional analysis is used to handle very large numbers of variables and many conventional dimensionless groups have come to be accepted, such as the Reynolds number and the Mach number. The choice of primary dimensions is, as we have seen, rather arbitrary, and a little experience is sometimes helpful. Obviously a certain amount of physical intuition is also necessary in selecting the right variables at the beginning. Nevertheless it is a powerful tool for the experimentalist and what it lacks in philosophical depth it makes up for in facility. Although we shall not pursue the matter here, we might note that dimensional analysis forms a basis for experimental model testing. This is a subject which is of great importance to engineers and worthy of study in its own right.

8

Time-series Analysis

A very important class of phenomena in science and engineering varies with time or some other parameter in an apparently unsystematic way. A few examples from engineering are radio noise, pressure variations in turbulence, heights of surface asperities, vibrations of vehicle structures, yearly flood levels. The fluctuations of these phenomena are essentially statistical in nature, and in the last generation or so a mathematical approach to their analysis has been worked out, mainly by communications engineers. Until recently the analysis was applied only to analogue signals which could be treated directly by electronic analogue techniques; this was because the computational work in treating a statistically representative series of discrete data was too great. This has all been changed by the advent of the digital computer, and time-series analysis is now an every-day tool of the practising scientist and engineer. The present chapter is an introduction to a few of the more elementary ideas of the subject, which we believe has not previously been treated at undergraduate level; even its simplest techniques are so powerful, however, and its use is becoming so widespread, that we do not feel a modern student-textbook on data analysis is complete without it.

8.1 Auto- and cross-correlation

Consider the signal shown in figure 8.1a. Superficially it resembles radio 'noise' as viewed on an oscilloscope screen. In fact it shows a vertical section through a ground surface nearly parallel with the lay, with the vertical scale exaggerated.

Figure 8.1b shows a section through the same surface taken at right angles to the lay. Clearly this and the previous figure are very different; for lack of a more precise description we might say that the first figure has a more 'open' texture than the second.

Is there any way in which we can obtain a more quantitative description?

Suppose we draw, from the mean line of the curve, a pair of ordinates separated by a horizontal distance λ. If λ is large (figure 8.2a) it is *unlikely* that these ordinates will lie on the same peak or valley. If we multiply them together

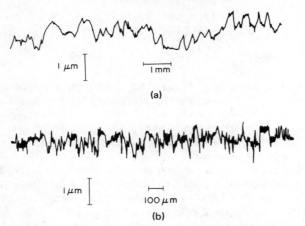

(a)

1 μm ⟩   1 mm

(b)

1 μm ⟩   100 μm

Figure 8.1. Two sections through a ground surface. (a) Nearly parallel to lay; (b) right angles to lay. Vertical scale exaggerated.

their product is equally likely to be positive or negative. If we add the products of a large number of such pairs of ordinates, therefore, their mean value will tend to zero.

If, on the other hand, we draw a pair of ordinates whose separation is small they are very likely to lie on the same peak or valley (figure 8.2b). They will therefore probably be of the same sign, whether positive or negative, and their product will be positive. The mean value of a large number of such products must be finite and also positive.

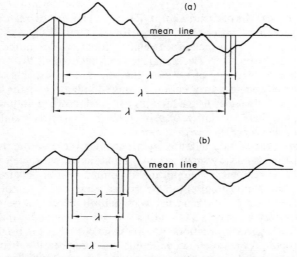

Figure 8.2. Pairs of signal amplitudes separated horizontally by distance (a) large, (b) small, compared with scale of signal variation.

We can thus define a statistic for a signal length L

$$R_{xx}(\lambda) = \frac{1}{L - \lambda} \int_0^{L-\lambda} f(x) f(x + \lambda) \, dx \tag{8.1}$$

which we can think of physically as a kind of figure of merit of geometrical relationship. It will vary continuously with λ, falling gradually to zero from an initial positive value at $\lambda = 0$. Its value at any given separation will be a measure of the average physical relationship of pairs of points with that separation; the length which it takes to decay to insignificance will be a measure of the average size of a peak.

The form of this statistic, which we have arrived at intuitively, may remind us of the covariance described in chapter 6. In fact equation 8.1 defines the *autocovariance function*. Its value for $\lambda = 0$ is the variance, the mean-square value of the signal (for an electrical signal, the average power)

$$R_{xx}(0) = \frac{1}{L} \int_0^L \{f(x)\}^2 \, dx \tag{8.2}$$

$$= \sigma_x^2 \tag{8.3}$$

$R_{xx}(\lambda)$ has the units of the square of the signal amplitude and can take any finite value. This is a disadvantage for a figure of merit which is to be used to compare the properties of signals of different powers. It is therefore convenient to convert it to dimensionless form by dividing by the variance

$$\rho_{xx}(\lambda) = R_{xx}(\lambda)/\sigma_x^2 \tag{8.4}$$

$$= \frac{1}{\sigma_x^2(L - \lambda)} \int_0^{L-\lambda} f(x) f(x + \lambda) \, dx \tag{8.5}$$

Equation 8.5 defines the *autocorrelation function*. The *autocorrelation coefficient* $\rho_{xx}(\lambda)$ remains within the range ± 1 for all λ and all signals.

Figures 8.3a and 8.3b show the autocorrelation functions computed for figures 8.1a and 8.1b respectively (we shall leave for the moment the practical problems of the actual computation). We see that this function is able to distinguish clearly between the two sections; correlation between pairs of heights measured at right angles to the lay falls off much more rapidly with increasing separation than correlation of pairs of heights measured parallel to the lay, which is in accordance with common sense.

An application of the autocorrelation function which is even more useful, is its ability to distinguish a very small periodic variation from a background of random variations of much greater amplitude. A communications engineer would describe this as ability to discriminate against a high signal-to-noise ratio. The autocorrelation function of a pure sine wave is itself a cosine wave of the same period; the autocorrelation function of a sine wave completely masked by random noise will still show a variation with the same period as the original sine wave. This is a property much used in communications engineering. Figure 8.4 shows an application in another field. A section through a machined surface appears purely random to the eye. Its autocorrelation function, however,

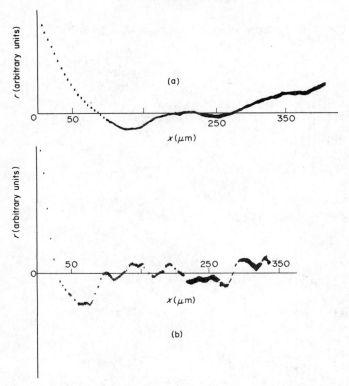

Figure 8.3. Autocorrelation function for signals of (a) figure 8.1a, (b) figure 8.1b.

discloses a pronounced periodicity. To the research worker this might be valuable evidence of the presence of an unwanted vibration in the structure of the machine tool.

Time series need not be continuous, as in the cases we have discussed. If the series is discrete a discrete form of equation 8.5 can be applied, and in fact continuous signals are often converted to discrete form for convenience of computation. Table 8.1 shows a rather unusual example of discrete time series[8]. This is a record of an experiment in which a student attempted to guess a sequence of twenty random numbers between 0 and 9 produced by a computer. Columns 1 and 4 of the table record respectively the student's guesses, which we shall call x, and the computer's random numbers which we shall call y. The auto-covariances were calculated for delays j ($j \equiv \lambda$) of 0, 1 and 2

$$R_{xx}(j) = \frac{1}{20-j} \sum_{i=1}^{20-j} (x_i - \bar{x})(x_{i+j} - \bar{x})$$

$$R_{yy}(j) = \frac{1}{20-j} \sum_{i=1}^{20-j} (y_i - \bar{y})(y_{i+j} - \bar{y})$$

(8.6)

($j = 0, 1, 2$)

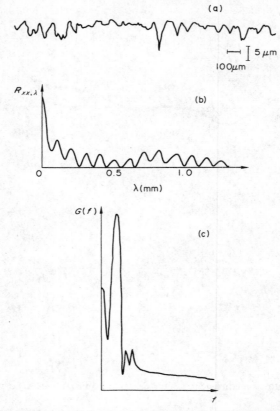

Figure 8.4. (a) Section through a turned surface. (b) Autocorrelation function revealing hidden periodicity of (a). (c) Power spectrum showing actual frequencies of periodicity[10].

Columns 3 and 6 of the table show the products of the residuals for $j = 2$, used to calculate the autocovariances for delay 2. The autocovariance of x thus compares pairs of successive guesses of the subject; a high value would suggest that the student was consciously or unconsciously guessing in a pattern. The autocovariance of y compares pairs of successive outputs of the random number generating algorithm; a high value would indicate that the numbers were not satisfactorily random.

The purpose of the experiment, however, was to assess the subject's ability to predict the computer's output. We therefore need some parameter which will compare the two time series. By analogy with our previous computations it might occur to us to sum the cross-products of the residuals

$$R_{xy}(j) = \frac{1}{20-j} \sum_{i=1}^{20-j} (x_i - \bar{x})(y_{i+j} - \bar{y}) \qquad (8.7)$$

Table 8.1. Subject's guesses x of 20 random numbers y: calculation of auto- and cross-correlation coefficients for delay 2

x	$x - \bar{x}$	$(x_i - \bar{x}) \times$ $(x_{i+2} - \bar{x})$	y	$(y - \bar{y})$	$(y_i - \bar{y}) \times$ $(y_{i+2} - \bar{y})$	$(x_i - \bar{x}) \times$ $(y_{i+2} - \bar{y})$
9	4.5		0	−4.55		
8	3.5		2	−2.55		
7	2.5	11.25	3	−1.55	7.0525	−6.975
6	1.5	5.25	3	−1.55	3.9525	−5.425
5	0.5	1.25	7	2.45	−3.7975	6.125
4	−0.5	−0.75	4	−0.55	0.8525	−0.825
3	−1.5	−0.75	7	2.45	6.0025	1.225
2	−2.5	1.25	8	3.45	−1.8975	−1.725
1	−3.5	5.25	7	2.45	6.0025	−3.675
0	−4.5	11.25	3	−1.55	−5.3475	3.875
0	−4.5	15.75	3	−1.55	−3.7975	5.425
1	−3.5	15.75	4	−0.55	0.8525	2.475
2	−2.5	11.25	7	2.45	−3.7975	−11.025
3	−1.5	5.25	2	−2.55	1.4025	8.925
4	−0.5	1.25	9	4.45	10.9025	−11.125
5	0.5	−0.75	5	0.45	−1.1475	−0.675
6	1.5	−0.75	4	−0.55	−2.4475	0.275
7	2.5	1.25	7	2.45	1.1025	1.225
8	3.5	5.25	6	1.45	−0.7975	2.175
9	4.5	11.25	0	−4.55	−11.1475	−11.375
90		99.50	91		3.945	−21.1

$$\bar{x} = \frac{\Sigma x}{n} = \frac{90}{20} = 4.50 \qquad \bar{y} = \frac{\Sigma y}{n} = \frac{91}{20} = 4.55$$

$$\sigma_x^2 = \frac{\Sigma(x - \bar{x})^2}{n} = \frac{165}{20} = 8.25 \qquad \sigma_y^2 = \frac{\Sigma(y - \bar{y})^2}{n} = \frac{128.95}{20} = 6.4475$$

$$\rho_{xx}(2) = \frac{\Sigma(x_i - \bar{x})(x_{i+2} - \bar{x})}{(n-2)\sigma_x^2} \qquad \rho_{yy}(2) = \frac{\Sigma(y_i - \bar{y})(y_{i+2} - \bar{y})}{(n-2)\sigma_y^2}$$

$$= \frac{99.50}{18 \times 8.25} = 0.6700 \qquad = \frac{3.945}{18 \times 6.4475} = 0.0340$$

$$\rho_{xy}(2) = \frac{\Sigma(x_i - \bar{x})(y_{i+2} - \bar{y})}{(n-2)\sigma_x\sigma_y} = \frac{-21.1}{18(8.25 \times 6.4475)^{1/2}} = -0.1607$$

We would now be comparing pairs of values of x and y. For zero delay this would of course be simply the covariance of x and y (see chapter 6)

$$R_{xy}(0) = \frac{1}{20} \sum_{i=1}^{20} (x_i - \bar{x})(y_i - \bar{y})$$

$$= \sigma_{xy}^2 \tag{8.8}$$

and hence would give us excellent information about the success of prediction.

The statistics for delays 1 and 2 would assess the subject's ability to guess 1 and 2 steps ahead of the computer.

$R_{xy}(j)$ is known as the *cross-covariance*. We make it dimensionless by dividing by the product of the individual standard deviations

$$\rho_{xy}(j) = R_{xy}(j)/\sigma_x \sigma_y \qquad (8.9)$$

Equation 8.9 defines the *cross-correlation coefficient*. The autocorrelation coefficients are formed similarly, by analogy with equation 8.4 for the continuous case

$$\rho_{xx}(j) = R_{xx}(j)/\sigma_{xx}^2 \qquad (8.10)$$
$$\rho_{yy}(j) = R_{yy}(j)/\sigma_{yy}^2 \qquad (8.11)$$

Table 8.2 shows the complete set of nine correlation coefficients for delays of 0, 1, 2. Note that both autocorrelation coefficients must have a value of unity for zero delay. The high value of $\rho_{xx}(1)$ suggests that the subject was in fact guessing in a pattern, while the low value of $\rho_{yy}(1)$ is satisfactory evidence that the random number generator is truly random. There is no indication from any of the values of the cross-correlation coefficient that the subject is in any way able to predict the output of the computer. This is a fortunate outcome for the manufacturers of fruit machines.

Table 8.2. Auto- and cross-correlation coefficients for the data of table 8.1

Delay j	$\rho_{xx}(j)$	$\rho_{yy}(j)$	$\rho_{xy}(j)$
0	1.0	1.0	-0.37
1	0.87	0.05	-0.24
2	0.67	0.03	-0.16

This conveniently introduces the idea of cross-correlation between two time series, which has a very much wider application than the above example.

For two functions x and y varying continuously with time, the continuous form of equation 8.7 becomes

$$R_{xy}(\lambda) = \frac{1}{L - \lambda} \int_0^{L-\lambda} x(t)\, y(t + \lambda)\, dt \qquad (8.12)$$

and the *cross-correlation function* is defined by

$$\rho_{xy}(\lambda) = R_{xy}(\lambda)/\sigma_x \sigma_y$$

$$= \frac{1}{\sigma_x \sigma_y (L - \lambda)} \int_0^{L-\lambda} x(t)\, y(t + \lambda)\, dt \qquad (8.13)$$

The cross-correlation function has a maximum possible value of unity, but it need not approach this value at $\lambda = 0$; in fact if two processes are completely independent their cross-correlation function need never deviate significantly from zero. It follows that a significant maximum or minimum on a cross-correlation function is evidence that the correlated series are not independent, and the delay λ at which this deviation occurs is a measure of the temporal relation between the events of the two series.

When a saturated vapour is in contact with a cold vertical smooth surface, the film of condensate which forms on the cold surface contains thickness variations of random amplitude and wavelength which travel down it. Because these thickness variations are of random amplitude and wavelength it is not easy to measure their average speed by conventional techniques. However, if the vertical surface is a glass plate and a light beam is directed transversely through it, the degree of attenuation as recorded by a photocell will be a measure of the instantaneous film thickness. Figures 8.5a and b are temporal records of the output of two photocells, responding to beams mounted one above the other. As the random disturbances in the film move downwards they will pass through and attenuate each beam in turn. Patterns of variation in the upstream beam will thus tend to be reproduced in the downstream beam a few instants later. This effect will be shown as a peak in the cross-correlation function (figure 8.5c).

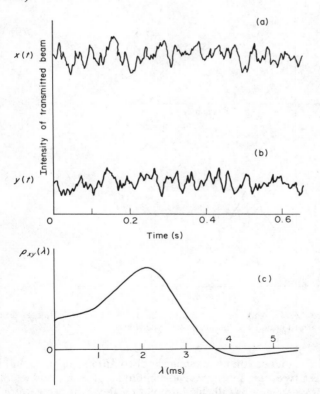

Figure 8.5. Output of (a) upstream, (b) downstream photocells measuring condensate film thickness. (c) Cross-correlation function of (a) with (b); time displacement of peak from origin represents average transit time of a travelling wave.

The temporal displacement of the peak from the origin will represent the time of transit of the train of disturbances from the upstream to the downstream beam. Since the beam separation is known the mean velocity of the waves may immediately be deduced. This is a measurement very difficult to make in any other way[9].

8.2   Power spectra

It is a familiar concept that a periodic signal, no matter how complex its waveform, can in principle be represented by Fourier analysis as the sum of a number of pure sinusoids. Because of the number of frequencies present, the number of Fourier terms needed in practice to describe a random signal is very large indeed, so large that if we plotted the amplitude of each term against its frequency the graph would appear as a continuous distribution (figure 8.6a).

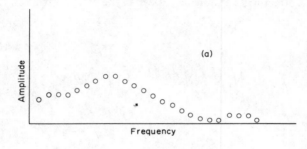

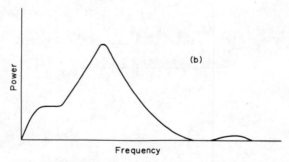

Figure 8.6.   (a) Amplitude spectrum; each point represents a Fourier term. (b) Corresponding continuous power spectrum.

By analogy with other continuous frequency-distributions (light, sound) we would call this a *spectrum,* in this case an amplitude spectrum, and we can imagine that it would give us valuable information about the presence or absence of particular frequencies in which we might be interested.

The labour involved in the computation of a large number of Fourier terms is unfortunately too great, even for a computer, to make an analysis of this kind practicable. Suppose, however, that instead of considering the amplitude at a particular frequency f we consider the *power* over a small range of frequencies from f to $f + \Delta f$

$$P(f, \Delta f) = \frac{1}{L} \int_0^L x^2(t, f, \Delta f)\, dt \tag{8.14}$$

where $x(t, f, \Delta f)$ represents the portion of $x(t)$ at frequencies between f and $f + \Delta f$. As Δf tends to the limit df we can define a function $G(f)$ analogous to a probability density, whose product with df will give us the power

$$G(f)\, df = \lim_{\Delta f \to df} P(f, df) \tag{8.15}$$

If we could compute $G(f)$ it would give us information about the frequency distribution which would be as adequate for our purposes as that derived from an amplitude spectrum. In fact $G(f)$ is just the Fourier transform of the auto-covariance function

$$G(f) = 4 \int_0^\infty R_{xx}(\lambda) \cos 2\pi f \lambda\, d\lambda \tag{8.16}$$

Equation 8.16 is the *Wiener–Khinchine relation* and is a fundamental identity of random-process theory. $G(f)$ is called the *power spectral density* and its variation with frequency is a *power spectrum* (figure 8.6b).

The area under the power spectrum between two given frequencies is the total power present in that frequency band (figure 8.7a)

$$\sigma_x^2|_{f_1-f_2} = \int_{f_1}^{f_2} G(f)\, df \tag{8.17}$$

The area under the whole power spectrum is the total power present in the signal

$$\sigma_x^2 = \int_0^\infty G(f)\, df \tag{8.18}$$

Two special cases of the power spectrum are worth mentioning. A signal which is a single pure sine wave must, of course, have all its power present in a single frequency. Its power spectrum therefore consists solely of a line of infinitesimal width at that frequency, that is, a Dirac delta function (figure 8.7b).

At the other extreme is a signal which contains all possible frequencies from zero to infinity at the same power. This is called *white noise,* and its power spectrum is a line extending to infinity parallel to the frequency axis. Such a signal cannot be realised in practice, but is truncated at upper and lower frequency limits; it is then called *band-pass white noise* (figure 8.7c).

For a practical example of the application of a power spectrum we return to the machined surface of figure 8.4. The autocorrelation function has already established the existence of a periodicity. The power spectrum of figure 8.4c discloses two peaks representing, no doubt, two resonant frequencies present in the machining process. Knowledge of these frequencies will help the engineer to identify and eliminate their source.

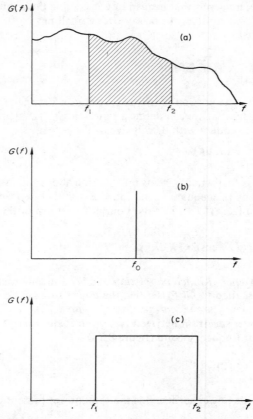

Figure 8.7. Power spectra. (a) Shaded area is power contained in signal frequencies between f_1 and f_2. (b) Power spectrum of pure sine wave of frequency f_0. (c) Power spectrum of band-pass white noise cut off at frequencies f_1 and f_2.

8.3   Measurement precautions

The measurement of random processes is itself a field of great scope, and we shall confine ourselves here to dealing with a few of the more obvious difficulties.

For the mathematical treatment of the previous section to apply, it is necessary that the signal should be both *stationary* and *ergodic.* Any sample length from an ergodic signal will have the same properties, within statistical limits, as any other sample. All ergodic signals are also stationary. *Non-stationary* random processes are mainly those where experimental conditions change during the period of measurement, and must be treated by special methods beyond the scope of this book. Fortunately a very large number of random processes of interest to the scientist and engineer can be treated as ergodic.

The first actual computations on random signals were made with analogue instruments: tape recorders with two playback heads of variable separation for correlation functions, and r.m.s. voltmeters with narrow band-pass filters for power spectra. Since the advent of digital computers, however, it has been increasingly the practice to convert continuous signals to discrete form, either directly on-line to the computer or through a recording device, to take advantage of the power and flexibility of the big machines. More recently still, hybrid computers have become available. These are portable instruments which can be connected directly to the signal and which carry out their computations partly by analogue and partly by digital circuitry.

If analogue-to-digital conversion (ADC) is involved in either of the above ways it is important to appreciate that this is not a completely straightforward process. The most common and most serious problem concerns the choice of the correct *sampling interval*. The ADC process measures the (nearly) instantaneous value of the signal at a large number of equal discrete intervals of time. The computer receives a succession of discrete numbers which taken together constitute a representation of the original signal. The possible pitfalls are best illustrated by figure 8.8, which shows the same signal sampled at two different intervals. In the first case the sampling interval is clearly too long and information concerning the highest frequencies is being lost (or worse, misinterpreted).

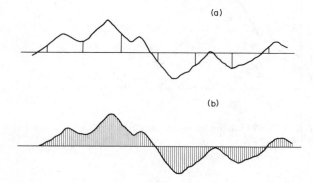

Figure 8.8. Different ways of sampling the same signal for analogue-to-digital conversion. (a) Sampling interval too long – higher frequencies are lost. (b) Sampling interval too short – redundant data.

In the second case the sampling interval is too short and the computer is being burdened with a large amount of redundant information. This may seem trivial, but time-series analysis is a lengthy business even for a big machine, and if a number of records, all with redundant information, are processed, it will be an expensive mistake.

If a signal is sampled at equal intervals of time λ_0 the highest frequency which the computer will subsequently detect is the *Nyquist frequency*

$$f_N = 1/2\lambda_0 \tag{8.19}$$

Higher frequencies which may exist in the signal will not, unfortunately, be filtered out but will reappear as spurious power at lower frequencies. This effect is known as *aliasing,* and can lead to gross misinterpretation of power spectra (figure 8.9). The problem can be solved by shortening the sampling

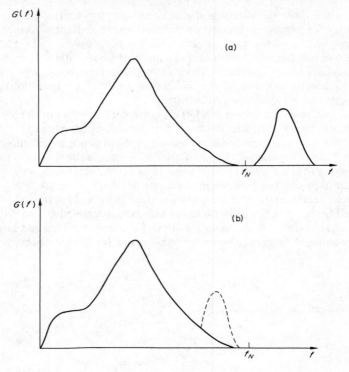

Figure 8.9. Effect of aliasing on power spectrum of a signal sampled at a Nyquist frequency f_N.

interval, with a consequent increase in volume of data for a given sample length and hence time and cost of computation. Often, also, limitations of the available equipment do not permit this solution. Alternatively, the signal can be passed prior to sampling through an analogue low-pass filter whose cut-off frequency is the Nyquist frequency. This is the preferred solution but of course one must make sure that the lost frequencies do not contain any information of importance to the experiment.

8.4   Computation

Having worked through the previous sections, we now have a time series which was either discrete to start with, as in the example of section 8.1, or has been converted to discrete form by the methods of the last section. Only in the most trivial cases is it possible to compute even correlation functions by hand, and manual computation of power spectra is quite out of the question; the remainder of this section will therefore assume that a digital computer is available to do the work.

At this stage the data will generally still be referred to some arbitrary zero. It is convenient to start by changing the reference datum to the mean value of the signal. If this changes with time, as it well may, the first stage of the data processing should fit a least-squares straight line (or polynomial if necessary) to the data to remove its upward or downward *trend* (figure 8.10).

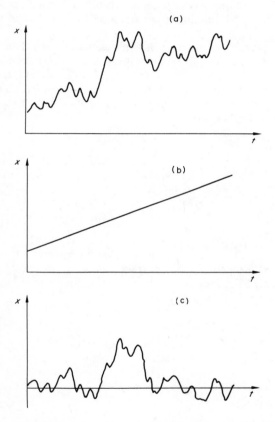

Figure 8.10. Removing trend from a signal by fitting a least-squares straight line. (a) Raw signal $x(t)$. (b) Least-squares straight line $at + b$. (c) Signal after trend removal: $x(t) - (at + b)$.

Computation of auto- and cross-correlation functions is straightforward, using the discrete form of the equations of section 8.1. The maximum delay $m(j = 0, 1 \ldots m)$, however, should not as a rule of thumb be greater than a tenth of the sample length, or the later values may not be entirely reliable.

Before we can compute a power spectrum it is necessary that the corresponding autocorrelation function be well behaved. If the interval in which it decays to zero is of the order of the maximum delay, too much power is present at low frequencies and the power spectrum will not yield accurate information.

If the information contained in the lower frequencies is essential there is nothing for it but to repeat the measurement with a longer sample length. If it is not, they can be removed with a high-pass *digital filter*. This again is too extensive a subject to be treated here, but it is worth remarking that in principle and often in practice digital filters are often superior to the corresponding analogue versions because they do not have to be physically realisable; an analogue filter can only work one way in time, but its digital version can take two bites at the same cherry by working backward as well as forward on the same record.

Computation of the power spectrum is a little more complicated than that of the correlation functions, as the raw estimate needs smoothing to remove 'noise' due to the effect of finite sample size. Only the final result will be quoted here. It turns out that the power spectral density can be computed only for m discrete frequencies corresponding to the m values of the auto-correlation function. The kth frequency

$$f_k = k f_N / m \tag{8.20}$$

$(k = 1, 2, \ldots m)$

and

$$G(f_k) = 2\lambda_0 \left\{ R_{xx}(0) + 2 \sum_{j=1}^{m-1} \frac{R_{xx}(j)}{2} \left(1 + \cos \frac{\pi j}{m}\right)\left(\cos \frac{\pi jk}{m}\right)\right\} \tag{8.21}$$

This is a lengthy computation, and is increasingly being replaced by the much quicker *fast Fourier-transform* (FFT), which operates directly on the signal itself. The theory of the FFT is far from straightforward, however, and interested readers are referred to specialist texts.

9

Further Statistical Distributions and Ideas

So far attention has been directed to the treatment of continuous variates. Consideration will now be given to a number of distributions which are useful when describing the behaviour of discrete data.

9.1 Binomial distribution

Perhaps the principal engineering application of this distribution is to production sampling. This is a subject which is treated fully in most textbooks on applied statistics and will not be pursued in detail here. However, the binomial distribution is a cornerstone of probability theory and a brief description of its properties is warranted. Suppose we conduct a series of trials in which the probability of a successful outcome is p and that of an unsuccessful outcome q. The distribution of successful outcomes in n trials may be shown to be described by the terms of the binomial expansion of $(q + p)^n$, hence the name of the distribution. It should be noted that as $q + p$ must be equal to unity, an event must either be successful or not; half measures are not allowed.

Using the combination notation, the expansion is

$$(q + p)^n = q^n + {}^nC_1 q^{n-1} p + {}^nC_2 q^{n-2} p^2 + \ldots + p^n$$

the rth term being

$${}^nC_{r-1} q^{n-r+1} p^{r-1}$$

To illustrate the application of the distribution, two examples will be considered.

Example 9.1

Suppose that three coins are tossed and a head is considered a success. Discuss the probability distribution of successful outcomes from a large number of tosses. The possible results of three tosses are listed below, where T signifies a tail and H a head.

T	T	T
T	T	H
T	H	T
H	T	T
T	H	H
H	H	T
H	T	H
H	H	H

There are eight possible outcomes. The probability of obtaining three heads is 1/8, as is the probability of three tails. The probability of obtaining two heads and one tail is 3/8, as is the probability of one head and two tails. Clearly, as $p = q = 1/2$, the distribution is symmetrical.

The expansion of $(q + p)^n$ gives

$$q^3 + {}^3C_1 q^2 p + {}^3C_2 qp^2 + p^3$$
$$= (\tfrac{1}{2})^3 + 3(\tfrac{1}{2})^2 \tfrac{1}{2} + 3(\tfrac{1}{2})(\tfrac{1}{2})^2 + (\tfrac{1}{2})^3$$
$$= 1/8 + 3/8 + 3/8 + 1/8$$

The first term, 1/8, is the probability of no successes (all tails); the second is the probability of one success (one head); the third is the probability of two heads and the last term is the probability of three heads occurring. This agrees with our original table of possible outcomes.

Example 9.2

It is known that 10 per cent of the output of a production process falls outside acceptable dimensional limits and is rejected. What proportion of defective parts is expected to occur in a number of samples of three items taken from a large production batch?

In this problem $p = 0.1$ and $n = 3$

Expanding the binomial expression as before we have

$$(q + p)^n = (0.9 + 0.1)^3$$
$$= 0.729 + 0.243 + 0.027 + 0.001$$

Hence the probability of the occurrence of

0 defectives = 0.729
1 defective = 0.243
2 defectives = 0.027
3 defectives = 0.001

The distribution is not now symmetrical. Also, it may seem a little surprising that although it is known that 10 per cent of the production batch is substandard, in 73 per cent of the samples no defective part appears. The unwary might well be tempted to make an over-optimistic assessment of the quality of the production batch.

Note. The evaluation of combination, ^nC_r, is given by

$$^nC_r = \frac{n(n-1) \ldots (n-r+1)}{r!}$$

$$= \frac{n!}{r!(n-r)!}$$

Readers not familiar with the notation may prefer to find the coefficients of the binomial series from Pascal's triangle.

Pascal's triangle

Value of n				Coefficients				
2				1	2	1		
3			1	3	3	1		
4		1	4	6	4	1		
5	1	5	10	10	5	1		

and so on, where each number is formed by adding those diagonally above it.

9.1.1 Mean and variance of binomial distribution

Equations 3.8 and 3.9 may be used to find the first and second moments of the distribution. The first gives the mean value $\bar{x}$, directly

$$\bar{x} = np$$

From the second moment and the parallel-axis equation 3.11 it can be shown that the variance is given by

$$\sigma^2 = npq$$

For the previous problem, example 9.2, where

$$p = 0.1, q = 0.9 \text{ and } n = 3$$
$$\bar{x} = np$$
$$= 0.3$$

and

$$\sigma^2 = npq$$
$$= 0.27$$

Notice that although the original data are integral the mean need not necessarily be so.

In example 9.2, the proportion of defectives in the bulk or population was assumed to be known. In many situations this is not the case and the problem is posed the other way round.

The object of taking a sample may well be to make an estimate of p. This is a much more difficult problem and entails a great deal of numerical work. If only a small sample is available the estimate is likely to be crude. Details of the methods used will not be pursued here. On the other hand, if circumstances permit a large number of samples to be taken, a histogram may be constructed. If this can be shown to be described by the binomial distribution, an appropriate value of p may be calculated from the relationship

$$p = \bar{x}/n$$

Before leaving the binomial distribution we recall that if p is close to 0.5, the distribution is symmetrical. For large values of n the binomial approximates closely to the normal distribution.

9.2   Poisson distribution

When the probability of a successful outcome in a large sample is very small, it will be shown that the distribution of occurrences is described by the terms of the expansion of $e^{-\bar{x}}e^{\bar{x}}$.

It has already been stated that for the binomial distribution the variance is smaller than the mean, as

$$\sigma^2 = npq < \bar{x} = np$$

If n is large and p small, q is also large; hence, the mean approaches the value of the variance. This new situation is described by the Poisson distribution which may be derived directly from the expanded form of the binomial.

Starting from the first few terms of the binomial distribution, we have

$$q^n + nq^{n-1}p + \frac{n(n-1)}{2!} q^{n-2}p^2$$

As n is large, $n \approx (n-1) \approx (n-2)$, etc.

The series may be rewritten as

$$q^n + nq^n p + \frac{n^2}{2!} q^n p^2$$

Substituting $\bar{x}/n$ for p and $1 - (\bar{x}/n)$ for q gives

$$\left(1 - \frac{\bar{x}}{n}\right)^n \left(1 + \bar{x} + \frac{\bar{x}^2}{2!} + \ldots\right)$$

In the limit as $n \to \infty$, the bracketed terms approach

$$e^{-\bar{x}}e^{\bar{x}} = 1$$

Hence, in situations where discrete events occur only rarely, their distribution is represented by the terms

$$e^{-\bar{x}}, \; e^{-\bar{x}}\bar{x}, \; e^{-\bar{x}}\frac{\bar{x}^2}{2!}, \; \ldots$$

with a mean and variance equal to np. For values of $\bar{x} < 1$, the distribution is J-shaped. For values of $\bar{x} > 1$, the distribution is skewed, but if $\bar{x} > 30$ it is almost symmetrical and closely approximates to a normal distribution with the same mean and variance.

To illustrate the use of the Poisson distribution, two examples will be considered.

Example 9.3

It is known that, on average, there is a demand for a particular replacement component once in 20 weeks. Assess the probabilities of a number of components being required in any period of one week.

Evidently the mean number of components required per week is 0.05. The probability is small and the Poisson distribution seems to be appropriate. The first three terms are shown tabulated.

Component required/week	0	1	2
Probability	$e^{-0.05}$	$0.05\,e^{-0.05}$	$\dfrac{0.05^2\,e^{-0.05}}{2!}$
Probability	0.951	0.048	0.001

The probability of no components being required in any one week is 0.951, of one component being required 0.048 and so on. It is not necessary to calculate e^{-n}, as tables are available.

Example 9.4

The average number of telephone calls on a certain line is 12 per hour; calculate the probabilities of 0, 1, 2, 3 or more calls being made in any period of five minutes.

The average number of calls in five minutes is 1. The first few terms of the distribution are tabulated.

Calls/5-minute period	0	1	2	3
Probability	e^{-1}	e^{-1}	$\dfrac{e^{-1}}{2!}$	$\dfrac{e^{-1}}{3!}$
Probability	0.3679	0.3679	0.1839	0.0613

The probabilities of 0, 1, 2 or 3 calls per 5 minutes are given above. The probability of 3 or more calls occurring is

$$1 - (0.3679 + 0.3679 + 0.1839)$$
$$= 0.0803$$

9.3   Chi-squared or χ^2 distribution

A full mathematical derivation of the χ^2 distribution is beyond the scope of this book. However, its application is not difficult. With certain restrictions the distribution may be adapted to test the significance of the difference between observed and expected frequencies of discrete data.

In such circumstances χ^2 is defined as

$$\chi^2 = \sum \frac{(O-E)^2}{E} \tag{9.1}$$

where O is an observed and E an expected frequency. Clearly, close agreement between observed and expected values results in a small value of χ^2.

The form of the distribution depends upon the number of independent squares present, that is, upon the number of degrees of freedom of the problem. This will be discussed in detail later in the chapter. Also the form of χ^2 given by equation 9.1 is only justified if the independent frequencies are greater than 5.

Applications of the distribution to testing 'Goodness-of-Fit' and Contingency Tables are illustrated by the following practical examples.

Examples 9.5

A Geiger tube is used to count the particles emitted from a weak phosphorus source. Emission is low, hence a Poisson distribution might reasonably be expected to apply. Table 9.1 gives the experimental results, showing the number of counts in 10-second intervals. Test the 'Goodness-of-Fit' of the experimental data with the Poisson law.

The mean number of counts per 10-second interval $\bar{x}$ is calculated from

$$\bar{x} = \frac{\Sigma(xO)}{\Sigma O}$$

$$= \frac{562}{71} = 7.9155$$

This value of the mean and the total frequency of events, that is, 71, is used to calculate the terms of the comparable distribution.

$$Ne^{-x} = 71e^{-7.9155}$$

$$= 259.22 \times 10^{-4}$$

hence, the rth term of the series is given by

$$259.22 \times 10^{-4} \frac{\bar{x}^{r-1}}{(r-1)!}$$

Earlier in this chapter it was shown that for a Poisson distribution the mean and variance are equal. As a first check on the suitability of the model the variance is calculated from the observed results and compared with the mean.

Table 9.1. Experimental counts of emission of
β-particles from a weak phosphorus source

No. of counts (x)	Observed frequency (O)
0	2
1	0
2	1
3	4
4	4
5	6
6	7
7	6
8	8
9	8
10	8
11	6
12	7
13	4
14	0

The variance s^2 and mean $\bar{x}$ are 10.16 and 7.92 respectively and as these are not equal the question arises: 'How good is the Poisson model?' Vague qualitati statements are undesirable and should be shunned.

If Poisson probability paper is available the observed results may be plotted and a further assessment of the suitability of the model made. The observed results are re-tabulated in table 9.2.

The last column lists the cumulative probability of the occurrence of at least one, two, three counts, and so on. It is formed from the previous column by adding terms starting from the bottom. The probabilities so found are plotted on the curved lines for constant values of x in figure 9.1.

Table 9.2. Processed data for emission of β-particle experiment

x	Frequency (O)	O/Total	Probability of at least x counts (P)
0	2	0.028	1.000
1	0	0	0.972
2	1	0.014	0.972
3	4	0.056	0.958
4	4	0.056	0.902
5	6	0.085	0.846
6	7	0.098	0.761
7	6	0.085	0.663
8	8	0.113	0.578
9	8	0.113	0.465
10	8	0.113	0.352
11	6	0.085	0.239
12	7	0.098	0.154
13	4	0.056	0.056
14 and over	0	0	0
Total	71		

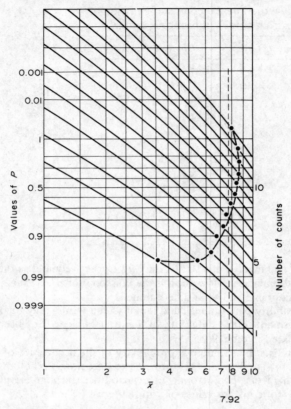

Figure 9.1. Experimental data of example 9.5 plotted on Poisson-probability paper.

Table 9.3. Processed data for emission of β-particle experiment

(x)	O	E	O	E	(O − E)	(O − E)²/E
0	2	0.0				
1	0	0.2				
2	1	0.8				
3	4	2.1				
4	4	4.2	11	7.3	3.7	1.87
5	6	6.7	6	6.7	− 0.7	0.07
6	7	8.9	7	8.9	− 1.9	0.41
7	6	10.0	6	10.0	− 4.0	1.60
8	8	9.9	8	9.9	− 1.9	0.36
9	8	8.7	8	8.7	− 0.7	0.06
10	8	6.9	8	6.9	1.1	0.17
11	6	5.0	6	5.0	1.0	0.20
12	7	3.3	11	7.0	4.0	2.29
13	4	2.0				
14	0	1.7				

$\Sigma O = 71$ $\chi^2 = 7.03$

If the observed frequencies agree exactly with those predicted by the Poisson law the results would lie on a vertical line at the mean value of 7.9. Clearly this is not the case in this instance. The points are disposed about a vertical line through the mean value and could possibly come from a Poisson distribution, the departures from the line being due to chance. The evidence is not conclusive and a further test is required.

A χ^2 test yields a quantitative measure in terms of the probability of the differences between observed and expected values being explained by chance. χ^2 is found from equation 9.1. A convenient arrangement of the calculation is shown in table 9.3.

In order to fulfil the requirement that independent frequencies should not be less than 5, the frequencies of four occurrences and less are grouped together. Similarly, those of 12 and greater are collected into a single cell. The second and third columns in table 9.3 headed O and E, refer to the original data, the next two show the observed and expected values after grouping. At the outset we assume the null-hypothesis that the observed and theoretical results come from the same Poisson distribution. As already pointed out, in calculating the theoretical frequencies the mean and total frequency of the observed results are employed, thus imposing two conditions or restrictions. Before proceeding to the tables the number of degrees of freedom ν, must be found. This is defined as

ν = number of groups or cells − number of restrictions and in this case

$$\nu = 9 - 2$$

$$= 7$$

Referring to the table of values of χ^2 given in the appendix it is seen that for 7 degrees of freedom

$$\chi^2 = 12.02$$

at a probability level of 0.1.

As the calculated value of 7.03 is considerably smaller than 12.02, the null-hypothesis is accepted as true. The difference between the observed and expected values is not in the least significant and could have occurred with a probability of greater than 10 per cent by chance alone. The Poissonian model is therefore acceptable.

9.3.1 When to accept or reject a null-hypothesis

The following rules are given as a guide.

If χ^2 is:	Difference between observed and expected values is:	Null-hypothesis is:
greater than 5 per cent	significant	probably false
greater than 1 per cent	most significant	almost certainly false REJECT
less than 5 per cent	not significant	probably true
less than 10 per cent	not in the least significant	very probably true ACCEPT

If χ^2 is very small, say less than the value given for $p = 95$ per cent, the null-hypothesis is almost too good to be true and should be treated with suspicion.

9.3.2 Degrees of freedom

The number of degrees of freedom of a problem has already been defined, in the last example, as the number of groups less the number of restrictions imposed. As we have seen, in the case of the Poisson distribution with the same mean and total frequency, two restrictions are applied. Although the normal distribution is continuous, the χ^2 'Goodness-of-Fit' test may still be used.

The procedure is to standardise the observed results by dividing by the standard deviation. Using the area under the normal curve in each class interval, which is readily obtainable from the tables, the expected results may be calculated for each cell. The observed and expected results will not, of course, be whole numbers. If the same mean standard deviation and total are used, three restrictions are imposed and

$$\nu = \text{(number of cells)} - 3$$

When testing data against the binomial distribution, if the probability of a success p, is given, then the only restriction is that the total frequencies agree; hence

$$\nu = \text{(number of cells)} - 1$$

If p has to be calculated from the data, the means and total frequencies must agree and

$$\nu = \text{(number of cells)} - 2$$

9.4 Contingency tables

The χ^2 distribution is also valuable in analysing so-called contingency problems. When a class corresponds to an attribute, the frequency table is known as a contingency table. The following examples illustrate a number of different types of problems of this kind.

Example 9.6

Suppose that four types of motor-car indicator-relay are tested over a period of six months and the number of failures are 5, 2, 4 and 1. Is there any real difference in the quality of the units?

Initially we shall assume a null-hypothesis that all units are equally good. The results are set out in tabular form.

Unit	O	E	$(O-E)^2/E$
A	5	3	4/3
B	2	3	1/3
C	4	3	1/3
D	1	3	4/3
Total	12	12	$4\frac{1}{3}$

χ^2 = 4.33 and

ν = number of classes − number of restrictions

= 4 − 1

= 3

as the total frequencies are made equal.

Referring to the tables we see that for 3 degrees of freedom, $\chi^2 = 6.25$ at the 10 per cent level. As our value is considerably less than this, the hypothesis is accepted. In spite of the variations in the breakages, we conclude that the evidence shows no real difference in the qualities of the units.

9.4.1 Yates' correction

If there are two groups only to be compared and the totals are made equal, the number of degrees of freedom is reduced to unity. In this case the numerical value of $(O - E)$, that is, the modulus of $(O - E)$, should be reduced by 1/2, thus decreasing the value of χ^2.

Example 9.7

Two groups of fifty fatigue specimens were subjected to the same tests. Group A specimens had their surfaces shot-blasted, whilst those of Group B were left in the machined condition. After a given period of time, ten of the specimens from Group A and twenty from Group B had failed. Is there any evidence that shot-blasting improves the fatigue resistance of the specimens?

Making a null-hypothesis that shot-blasting had had no effect, we expect the failure rate of Group A to be the same as that of Group B.
Tabulating the results:

	Group A (O)	Group B (E)	(O − E)	(O − E) corrected	(O − E)²/E
Failed	10	20	− 10	9½	4.51
Survived	40	30	10	9½	3.01
Total	50	50		$\chi^2 = 7.51$	

Hence

χ^2 = 7.51

From the tables we see that χ^2 is only 6.63 at 1 per cent. Evidently the effect of shot-blasting on fatigue life is highly significant and the difference in the results is extremely unlikely to have occurred by chance.

9.4.2. (h × k) contingency table

Suppose we wish to examine if there is any significant relationship between two sets of attributes. This is done by drawing up a $(h \times k)$ contingency table, where h is the number of one type of attribute and k the number of the other. Again the procedure is illustrated by an example.

Example 9.8

The table shows the result of a survey of the natural hair colouring of the wives of a group of eighteen engineers and twelve other men drawn from other different, but equally estimable professions.

	Engineers	Others
Blondes	8	4
Redheads	5	5
Brunettes	5	3

Is there any evidence here that blondes prefer engineers?

Firstly, rewrite the table summing the rows and columns.

	Engineers	Others	Totals
Blondes	8	4	12
Redheads	5	5	10
Brunettes	5	3	8
Totals	18	12	30

We now calculate the expected probability for each combination. For example, from a total of thirty men with thirty wives, the expected frequency of an engineer having a blonde wife is given by

$$30 \times 12/30 \times 18/30 \ = \ 7.2$$

Similarly, we complete the expected frequency table below

	Engineers	Others
Blondes	7.2	4.8
Redheads	6.0	4.0
Brunettes	4.8	3.2

We are now able to write down the observed and expected frequencies in a systematic order.

O	E	$(O-E)$	$(O-E)^2$	$(O-E)^2/E$
8	7.2	0.8	0.64	0.089
4	4.8	−0.8	0.64	1.333
5	6.0	−1.0	1.0	0.167
5	4.0	1.0	1.0	0.125
5	4.8	0.2	0.04	0.008
3	3.2	−0.2	0.04	0.012

$$\chi^2 = 1.734$$

The number of degrees of freedom ν is given by

$$\nu = (h-1)(k-1)$$

As the totals of the rows and the columns are equal for the observed and expected frequencies, two restrictions are imposed. In this case

$$\nu = (2-1)(3-1)$$
$$= 2$$

The value of χ^2 at the 10 per cent level is given in the tables as 4.61. Hence the differences in our survey are not in the least significant and the null hypothesis must regretfully be accepted: there is no evidence that blondes prefer engineers.

9.5 Weibull distribution

Since it was first suggested by Weibull in 1951, this distribution has found many engineering applications including the description of a wide range of fatigue phenomena. One of the best known of these is to the prediction of the endurance life of ball and roller bearings. If we exclude catastrophic failures due to accidents or poor design, the life of roller bearings is limited by the generation of sub-surface fatigue cracks. Eventually such cracks extend to the surface and become apparent when flaking or spalling occurs. Roller bearings are now universally marketed to a specification based upon the Weibull distribution. Sales catalogues quote a B_{10}-life for a particular load and speed; this means that in the period of the B_{10}-life it is estimated that not more than 10 per cent of a large number of bearings would fail due to surface fatigue under such conditions.

Before developing the distribution we might note that fatigue tests are expensive and time consuming and therefore usually involve only a limited number of specimens. This leads to problems, not exclusively associated with fatigue testing, but which occur whenever we are faced with a small sample. When a large sample is available it is possible to investigate the character of the population straightforwardly by drawing a histogram as described in section 3.1. If the sample is small the shape of the histogram is very sensitive to the choice of class interval and it is more satisfactory to work with the cumulative distribution. The usual procedure is to construct the cumulative distribution by plotting the observations as abscissae and the *rank* of the observations as ordinates.

9.5.1   Ranking

Suppose that we have a small sample of five specimens which are to be tested to destruction. The first failure represents 20 per cent of the sample destroyed. Can we deduce from this that 20 per cent of the population would, if tested, fail in the same period of time? Clearly this may not be so and we need a statistical method of estimating the fraction of the population represented by each of the five failures in the sample. In other words we must determine the rank of each failed specimen.

9.5.2   Median ranks

Consider a number of samples of five items taken from a population with a known frequency distribution. The times to failure for the first specimen from each sample will be distributed randomly. The median of these lives is called the median rank of the first failure. This means that we estimate that 50 per cent of such failures in the population would occur at a shorter life and 50 per cent at a longer life than the median. For a sample of five the median rank of the first failure turns out to be 12.94 per cent. Similarly the ranks of the second and subsequent failures may be calculated. Those readers interested in the details of the calculations are referred to a paper on the subject by Johnson.

A table in appendix A gives the ranks of samples of up to ten specimens. If a table is not available the rank may be calculated from the approximation

$$\text{Median rank} = \frac{j - 0.3}{n - 0.4}$$

where

j = failure order number
n = sample size

9.5.3   Other ranks

In a similar manner other ranks such as the 5 per cent and 95 per cent may be calculated. For example, the 5 per cent rank for the first failure from a sample of five specimens is 1 per cent. This means that only in 5 per cent of cases the lowest specimens would represent less than 1 per cent of the population. The 95 per cent rank for the lowest of five specimens is 45 per cent which means that in 95 per cent of cases the lowest of five would represent as much as 45 per cent of the population.

The 5 and 95 per cent ranks for up to ten specimens are given in a table in appendix A.

9.6   The Weibull probability-density and cumulative-probability functions

The probability-density function for the Weibull distribution is given by

$$p(x) = \frac{\beta}{\eta} \left(\frac{x - x_0}{\eta} \right)^{\beta - 1} \exp - \left(\frac{x - x_0}{\eta} \right)^{\beta} \tag{9.2}$$

this includes three constants β, x_0 and η.

β is called the Weibull slope and gives a measure of the scatter of the experimental points.

x_0 is the starting point of the distribution (in some cases it may be taken as zero) and η is a characteristic value.

The shape of the distribution varies greatly with changes in the value of β. Figure 9.2 shows a number of typical curves. When $\beta = 1$ the distribution is exponential, when $\beta = 2$ it is similar to the well-known Rayleigh distribution which describes the peaks of a narrow-band random process (see chapter 8) and when $\beta = 3.46$ it is almost normal.

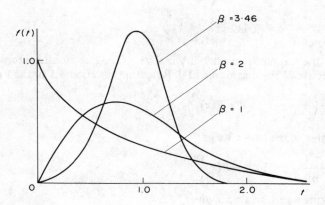

Figure 9.2. Typical probability-density curves for the Weibull distribution.

Let

$$y = \left(\frac{x - x_0}{\eta}\right)^\beta \qquad (9.3)$$

differentiating we get

$$\frac{dy}{dx} = \frac{\beta}{\eta}\left(\frac{x - x_0}{\eta}\right)^{\beta-1} \qquad (9.4)$$

substituting equations 9.3 and 9.4 into equation 9.2 gives

$$p(x) = \frac{dy}{dx}\, e^{-y}$$

For any probability distribution

$$P(x) = \int_{x_0}^{x} p(x)\, dx$$

therefore, in this case

$$P(x) = \int_{0}^{y} e^{-y}\, dy$$

integrating gives

$$P(x) = [-e^{-y}]_0^y$$

and substituting back for y and putting in the limits we have

$$P(x) = 1 - \exp -\left(\frac{x - x_0}{\eta}\right)^\beta \tag{9.5}$$

Note that when $(x - x_0) = \eta$

$$P(x) = 1 - e^{-1}$$

$$= \frac{e - 1}{e} = 0.632$$

That is to say, the cumulative probability is always 0.632 at the characteristic value η irrespective of the magnitude of β. Rewriting equation 9.5 in the form

$$\exp -\left(\frac{x - x_0}{\eta}\right)^\beta = 1 - P(x)$$

taking logarithms to the base e we get

$$-\left(\frac{x - x_0}{\eta}\right)^\beta = \ln\left\{1 - P(x)\right\}$$

and finally taking logarithms again gives

$$\ln \ln \left\{\frac{1}{1 - P(x)}\right\} = \beta \ln(x - x_0) - \beta \ln \eta \tag{9.6}$$

which may be written as

$$Y = Ax + B$$

This is a straight-line law with a slope A which is equal to the Weibull slope β. Special probability paper can be obtained which has a logarithmic scale on the abscissa and an ordinate scale which converts $P(x)$ into $\ln \ln 1/(1 - P(x))$.

9.7   Life fatigue testing

If $P(x)$ is the cumulative failure of a component, the ordinates on Weibull paper represent the percentage failed while the abscissa represents the corresponding life. The median ranks of the specimens are used to plot the ordinates.

Consider an example concerned with the endurance life of ball-bearings.

Example 9.9

Five ball-bearings subjected to a constant radial load of 4000 N were run at a constant inner race speed of 10 r.p.s. The cycles to failure were 1.2, 3.0, 4.5, 7.2 and 9.9 $\times$ 10^6. Examine the results of this series of trials by means of the Weibull distribution.

Table 9.4. Results of constant-speed, constant-load bearing-test

Specimen number	Life to failure in 10^6 cycles	Median rank
1	1.2	12.94
2	3.0	31.47
3	4.5	50.00
4	7.2	68.53
5	9.9	87.06

The lives are arranged in increasing order of failure and a median rank assigned to each specimen, as in table 9.4 (see appendix A for median ranks).

Life is plotted on the abscissa of Weibull-probability paper and the corresponding median rank on the ordinate. The best line is drawn through the points. It is often possible to do this by eye, but if the scatter is large the methods of fitting a best line described in chapter 6 may be employed.

In this example the points lie close to a straight line and we have no problem. However, if this were not so it would indicate one of two things: either the data is not described by the Weibull distribution or that x_0 the initial point of the distribution is not zero. If the points lie on a smooth curve a value for x_0 other than zero should be assumed and the data replotted. A number of trials, each time refining the value of x_0, should straighten the curve into a line.

Having plotted the line we require the Weibull slope. This will be the same as the geometrical slope only if the paper is constructed so that a value of β equal to 1 gives a slope of $45°$. Many commercially available papers are not to this scale so that β must either be calculated, or use made of the estimating point and the construction indicated in figure 9.3. This consists of drawing a perpendicular to the Weibull line through the estimating point. β is read directly from the horizontal β scale.

In our case

$$\beta = 1.3$$

This may readily be checked by calculation. From equation 9.6 we have

$$\ln \ln \left\{ \frac{1}{1-P(x_1)} \right\} - \beta \ln x_1 = \ln \ln \left\{ \frac{1}{1-P(x_2)} \right\} - \beta \ln x_2$$

where x_0 is zero.

Choosing two convenient points on the line, say

$$P(x_1) = 0.1 \text{ when } x_1 = 10^6$$
$$P(x_2) = 0.87 \text{ when } x_2 = 10^7$$

we get

$$\ln \ln \frac{1}{0.9} - 13.82\beta = \ln \ln \frac{1}{0.13} - 16.12\beta$$

therefore

$$\beta = 1.295$$

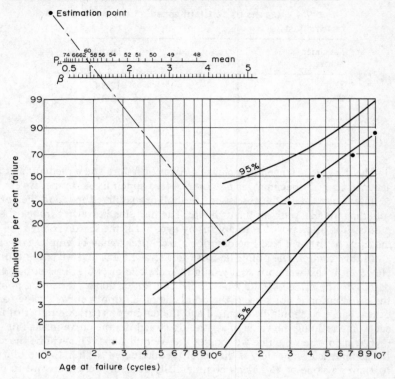

Figure 9.3. Cumulative probability of failure as a function of age at failure; data of table plotted on Weibull-probability paper showing 90 per cent confidence band.

The characteristic life η corresponds to the 63.2 per cent failure point and may be read directly from the graph; this gives

$$\eta = 5.8 \times 10^6 \text{ cycles}$$

As the distribution is not symmetrical the mean and median are not equal. The mean may be read from the horizontal mean scale. In our case the mean is 59.5 per cent and from the graph the mean life is 5.5×10^6 cycles.

We have already mentioned that a figure of interest to bearing engineers is the B_{10}-life. Reading directly from the graph the B_{10}-life is 1×10^6 cycles. We might note in passing that the mean life is roughly five times the B_{10}-life.

9.7.1 Confidence limits

In figure 9.3 in addition to the Weibull line curves are drawn through the 5 and 95 per cent rank values. These lines represent the 90 per cent confidence limits.

The B_{50}-life from the Weibull line is 4.4×10^6 cycles. From the confidence band we see that the limits are 1.65 to 9.2×10^6 cycles. This is a fairly wide range as one might expect for a small sample of five specimens.

We see that the lower limit of reliability, that is, the 95 per cent rank line, does not extend below about $P(x) = 44$ per cent and hence cannot be used directly to find for example the B_{10} confidence limits. Alternative methods are available but are beyond the scope of this book.

9.7.2 Sudden-death testing

A great deal of time may be saved by the sudden-death method of testing for endurance of life.

Suppose that a batch of forty specimens is available for testing. This is divided into say eight batches of five and a test started on the first batch. As soon as the first specimen fails further running on this batch is stopped and the second batch run. The times to the first failure from each batch is noted.

We now have eight values for the first failure from batches of five specimens. From the table of median ranks we see that the first failure from five cluster around a median of 12.94 of the population.

The values for the eight failures are plotted on Weibull paper in increasing order of median rank for a sample size of eight. The B_{50}-point on the line through the points is taken as the best estimated median value of the $B_{12.94}$-life. A line is dropped down the ordinate to meet a horizontal line through the 12.94 point as shown in figure 9.4. This gives a point on the estimated failure line for the population. A line drawn parallel to the original line through the point represents the failure line for the population to the same accuracy as would be obtained by testing the whole batch of forty specimens.

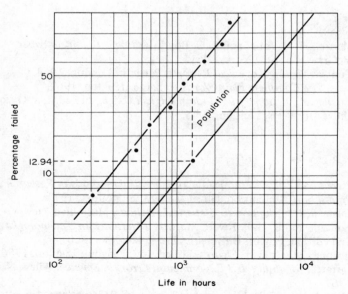

Figure 9.4. Typical sudden-death test showing the first failures from eight batches of five specimens each plotted on Weibull paper.

Further Reading

Chapter 1

O. L. Davies, *Design and Analysis of Industrial Experiments,* 2nd edition,
    Hafner, New York, 1956.
J. Holman, *Experimental Methods for Engineers,* McGraw-Hill, New York, 1966.
H. Schenck, *Theories of Engineering Experimentation,* 2nd edition, McGraw-Hill,
    New York, 1968.
S. D. Probert, J. P. Marsden and T. W. Holmes, *Experimental Method and
    Measurement,* Heinemann, London, 1971.

Chapter 2

D. H. Menzel, H. M. Jones and L. G. Boyd, *Writing a Technical Paper,*
    McGraw-Hill, New York, 1961.
B. M. Cooper, *Writing Technical Reports,* Penguin, London, 1964.
E. Gowers, *The Complete Plain Words,* Penguin, London, 1962.
H. W. Fowler, *A Dictionary of Modern English Usage,* 2nd edition, Oxford
    University Press, London, 1965.

Chapter 3

O. L. Davies and P. L. Goldsmith (eds), *Statistical Methods in Research and
    Production,* 4th edition, Oliver & Boyd, Edinburgh, 1972.
H. J. Halstead, *Introduction to Statistical Methods,* Macmillan, New York, 1966.
C. G. Paradine and B. H. P. Rivett, *Statistical Methods for Technologists,*
    2nd edition, English Universities Press, London, 1960.
M. J. Moroney, *Facts from Figures,* 3rd edition, Penguin, London, 1956.
L. G. Parratt, *Probability and Experimental Errors in Science,* Wiley, New York,
    1961.
E. T. Whittaker and J. Robinson, *The Calculus of Observations,* 4th edition,
    Blackie, London, 1944.

Chapters 4, 5 and 6

As for chapter 3.

Chapter 7

H. L. Langhaar, *Dimensional Analysis and Theory of Models,* Wiley, New York, 1951.

R. C. Pankhurst, *Dimensional Analysis and Scale Factors,* Chapman & Hall, London, 1964.

Chapter 8

J. S. Bendat and A. G. Piersol, *Random Data: Analysis and Measurement Procedures,* Wiley-Interscience, New York, 1971.

R. B. Blackman and J. W. Tukey, *The Measurement of Power Spectra,* Dover Press, New York, 1958.

J. M. Craddock, *Statistics in the Computer Age,* English Universities Press, London, 1968.

Chapter 9

As for chapter 3 with the addition of

G. J. Johnson, The median ranks of sample values in their population with an application to certain fatigue studies. *Industrial Mathematics,* 2 (1951), 1—9

C. Lipson and N. J. Sheth, *Statistical Design and Analysis of Engineering Experiments,* McGraw-Hill, New York, 1973.

R. A. Mitchell, Introduction to Weibull analysis. *Pratt and Whitney Report.* No. 3001, 1967.

References

1. A. Bennett and G. R. Higginson. Hydrodynamic lubrication of soft solids. *J. mech. Engng Sci.* **12** (1970), 218–22.
2. T. R. Thomas, Correlation analysis of the structure of a ground surface, *Proc. 13th Int. Machine Tool Design and Research Conf.*, Macmillan, London, 1973, 303–6.
3. T. R. Thomas and S. D. Probert. Establishment of contact parameters from surface profiles, *J. Phys.* **D3** (1970), 277–89.
4. E. Rabinowicz. *Friction and Wear of Materials*, Wiley, New York, 1965.
5. T. R. Thomas and S. D. Probert. Correlations for thermal contact conductance *in vacuo, Trans. Am. Soc. mech. Engrs* **94C** (1972), 276–81.
6. D. Dowson and G. R. Higginson, *Elasto-Hydrodynamic Lubrication,* Pergamon Press, London, 1966.
7. J. A. Greenwood. Presentation of elastohydrodynamic film-thickness results. *J. mech. Engng Sci.* **11** (1969), 128–32.
8. T. R. Thomas. Precognition experiments with a time-sharing computer (in the press).
9. D. Rigg and G. Drummond. Private communication.
10. J. Peklenik. New developments in surface characterization and measurements by means of random process analysis. *Proc. Inst. Mech. Engrs* **182,** Part 3k (1967–8), 108–26.

Appendix A:

Statistical Tables

Table A1 Cumulative normal distribution

Shaded area Q is the probability that a value of t from a normal population will be less than or equal to v (see section 4.1).

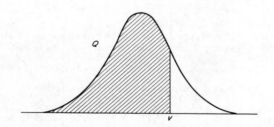

v	0	1	2	3	4	5	6	7	8	9
0·0	5000	5040	5080	5120	5160	5199	5239	5279	5319	5359
0·1	5398	5438	5478	5517	5557	5596	5636	5675	5714	5753
0·2	5793	5832	5871	5910	5948	5987	6026	6064	6103	6141
0·3	6179	6217	6255	6293	6331	6368	6406	6443	6480	6517
0·4	6554	6591	6628	6664	6700	6736	6772	6808	6844	6879
0·5	6915	6950	6985	7019	7054	7088	7123	7157	7190	7224
0·6	7257	7291	7324	7357	7389	7422	7454	7486	7517	7549
0·7	·7580	7611	7642	7673	7704	7734	7764	7794	7823	7852
0·8	7881	7910	7939	7967	7995	8023	8051	8078	8106	8133
0·9	8159	8186	8212	8238	8264	8289	8315	8340	8365	8389
1·0	8413	8438	8461	8485	8508	8531	8554	8577	8599	8621
1·1	8643	8665	8686	8708	8729	8749	8770	8790	8810	8830
1·2	8849	8869	8888	8907	8925	8944	8962	8980	8997	9015
1·3	9032	9049	9066	9082	9099	9115	9131	9147	9162	9177
1·4	9192	9207	9222	9236	9251	9265	9279	9292	9306	9319
1·5	9332	9345	9357	9370	9382	9394	9406	9418	9429	9441
1·6	9452	9463	9474	9484	9495	9505	9515	9525	9535	9545
1·7	9554	9564	9573	9582	9591	9599	9608	9616	9625	9633
1·8	9641	9649	9656	9664	9671	9678	9686	9693	9699	9706
1·9	9713	9719	9726	9732	9738	9744	9750	9756	9761	9767
2·0	9772	9778	9783	9788	9793	9798	9803	9808	9812	9817
2·1	9821	9826	9830	9834	9838	9842	9846	9850	9854	9857
2·2	9861	9865	9868	9871	9875	9878	9881	9884	9887	9890
2·3	9893	9896	9898	9901	9904	9906	9909	9911	9913	9916
2·4	9918	9920	9922	9925	9927	9929	9931	9932	9934	9936
2·5	9938	9940	9941	9943	9945	9946	9948	9949	9951	9952
2·6	9953	9955	9956	9957	9959	9960	9961	9962	9963	9964
2·7	9965	9966	9967	9968	9969	9970	9971	9972	9973	9974
2·8	9974	9975	9976	9977	9977	9978	9979	9979	9980	9981
2·9	9981	9982	9982	9983	9984	9984	9985	9985	9986	9986
3·0	9987	9987	9987	9988	9988	9989	9989	9989	9990	9990
3·1	9990	9991	9991	9991	9992	9992	9992	9992	9993	9993
3·2	9993	9993	9994	9994	9994	9994	9994	9995	9995	9995
3·3	9995	9995	9995	9996	9996	9996	9996	9996	9996	9997
3·4	9997	9997	9997	9997	9997	9997	9997	9997	9997	9998

v	0·6745	1·6449	1·9600	2·5758	3·0902	3·2905	4·8916
$2\{1-A(v)\}$	0·50	·0·10	0·05	0·01	0·002	0·001	10^{-6}

Table A2 Student's t

Shaded area $Q = Q_1 + Q_2$ is the probability that a value of $|t|$ calculated with ν degrees of freedom will exceed $|t|$ if both samples are from the same population (see section 5.3.1).

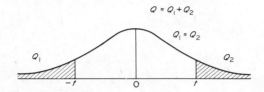

ν	Probability of deviation numerically greater than t				
	0·1	0·05	0·01	0·002	0·001
1	6·314	12·71	63·66	318·3	636·6
2	2·920	4·303	9·925	22·33	31·60
3	2·353	3·182	5·841	10·22	12·94
4	2·132	2·776	4·604	7·173	8·610
5	2·015	2·571	4·032	5·893	6·859
6	1·943	2·447	3·707	5·208	5·959
7	1·895	2·365	3·499	4·785	5·405
8	1·860	2·306	3·355	4·501	5·041
9	1·833	2·262	3·250	4·297	4·781
10	1·812	2·228	3·169	4·144	4·587
11	1·796	2·201	3·106	4·025	4·437
12	1·782	2·179	3·055	3·930	4·318
13	1·771	2·160	3·012	3·852	4·221
14	1·761	2·145	2·977	3·787	4·140
15	1·753	2·131	2·947	3·733	4·073
16	1·746	2·120	2·921	3·686	4·015
17	1·740	2·110	2·898	3·646	3·965
18	1·734	2·101	2·878	3·611	3·922
19	1·729	2·093	2·861	3·579	3·883
20	1·725	2·086	2·845	3·552	3·850
21	1·721	2·080	2·831	3·527	3·819
22	1·717	2·074	2·819	3·505	3·792
23	1·714	2·069	2·807	3·485	3·767
24	1·711	2·064	2·797	3·467	3·745
25	1·708	2·060	2·787	3·450	3·725
26	1·706	2·056	2·779	3·435	3·707
27	1·703	2·052	2·771	3·421	3·690
28	1·701	2·048	2·763	3·408	3·674
29	1·699	2·045	2·756	3·396	3·659
30	1·697	2·042	2·750	3·385	3·646
40	1·684	2·021	2·704	3·307	3·551
60	1·671	2·000	2·660	3·232	3·460
120	1·658	1·980	2·617	3·163	3·373
∞	1·645	1·960	2·576	3·090	3·291

118 ANALYSIS AND PRESENTATION OF EXPERIMENTAL RESULTS

Table A3 Fisher's F-distribution

Shaded area Q is the probability that a value of F calculated with ν_1 and ν_2 degrees of freedom $(F > 1)$ will exceed F_Q for two samples from the same population (see section 5.3.2).

Probability of exceeding F	ν_2 \ ν_1	1	2	3	4	5	6	7	8	10	12	24	∞
0·05	1	161	200	216	225	230	234	237	239	242	244	249	254
0·025		648	800	864	900	922	937	948	957	969	977	997	1018
0·01		4052	5000	5403	5625	5764	5859	5928	5981	6056	6106	6235	6366
0·05	2	18·5	19·0	19·2	19·3	19·4	19·4	19·4	19·4	19·4	19·4	19·5	19·5
0·025		38·5	39·0	39·2	39·2	39·3	39·3	39·4	39·4	39·4	39·4	39·5	39·5
0·01		98·5	99·0	99·2	99·2	99·3	99·3	99·4	99·4	99·4	99·4	99·5	99·5
0·05	3	10·13	9·55	9·28	9·12	9·01	8·94	8·89	8·85	8·79	8·74	8·64	8·53
0·025		17·4	16·0	15·4	15·1	14·9	14·7	14·6	14·5	14·4	14·3	14·1	13·9
0·01		34·1	30·8	29·5	28·7	28·2	27·9	27·7	27·5	27·2	27·1	26·6	26·1
0·05	4	7·71	6·94	6·59	6·39	6·26	6·16	6·09	6·04	5·96	5·91	5·77	5·63
0·025		12·22	10·65	9·98	9·60	9·36	9·20	9·07	8·98	8·84	8·75	8·51	8·26
0·01		21·2	18·0	16·7	16·0	15·5	15·2	15·0	14·8	14·5	14·4	13·9	13·5
0·05	5	6·61	5·79	5·41	5·19	5·05	4·95	4·88	4·82	4·74	4·68	4·53	4·36
0·025		10·01	8·43	7·76	7·39	7·15	6·98	6·85	6·76	6·62	6·52	6·28	6·02
0·01		16·26	13·27	12·06	11·39	10·97	10·67	10·46	10·29	10·05	9·89	9·47	9·02
0·05	6	5·99	5·14	4·75	4·53	4·39	4·28	4·21	4·15	4·06	4·00	3·84	3·67
0·025		8·81	7·26	6·60	6·23	5·99	5·82	5·70	5·60	5·46	5·37	5·12	4·85
0·01		13·74	10·92	9·78	9·15	8·75	8·47	8·26	8·10	7·87	7·72	7·31	6·88
0·05	7	5·59	4·74	4·35	4·12	3·97	3·87	3·79	3·73	3·64	3·57	3·41	3·23
0·025		8·07	6·54	5·89	5·52	5·29	5·12	4·99	4·90	4·76	4·67	4·42	4·14
0·01		12·25	9·55	8·45	7·85	7·46	7·19	6·99	6·84	6·62	6·47	6·07	5·65

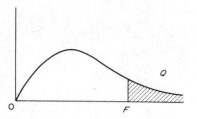

n_2	Q												
8	0·05	2·93	3·12	3·28	3·35	3·44	3·50	3·58	3·69	3·84	4·07	4·46	5·32
	0·025	3·67	3·95	4·20	4·30	4·43	4·53	4·65	4·82	5·05	5·42	6·06	7·57
	0·01	4·86	5·28	5·67	5·81	6·03	6·18	6·37	6·63	7·01	7·59	8·65	11·26
9	0·05	2·71	2·90	3·07	3·14	3·23	3·29	3·37	3·48	3·63	3·86	4·26	5·12
	0·025	3·33	3·61	3·87	3·96	4·10	4·20	4·32	4·48	4·72	5·08	5·71	7·21
	0·01	4·31	4·73	5·11	5·26	5·47	5·61	5·80	6·06	6·42	6·99	8·02	10·56
10	0·05	2·54	2·74	2·91	2·98	3·07	3·14	3·22	3·33	3·48	3·71	4·10	4·96
	0·025	3·08	3·37	3·62	3·72	3·85	3·95	4·07	4·24	4·47	4·83	5·46	6·94
	0·01	3·91	4·33	4·71	4·85	5·06	5·20	5·39	5·64	5·99	6·55	7·56	10·04
11	0·05	2·40	2·61	2·79	2·85	2·95	3·01	3·09	3·20	3·36	3·59	3·98	4·84
	0·025	2·88	3·17	3·43	3·53	3·66	3·76	3·88	4·04	4·28	4·63	5·26	6·72
	0·01	3·60	4·02	4·40	4·54	4·74	4·89	5·07	5·32	5·67	6·22	7·21	9·65
12	0·05	2·30	2·51	2·69	2·75	2·85	2·91	3·00	3·11	3·26	3·49	3·89	4·75
	0·025	2·72	3·02	3·28	3·37	3·51	3·61	3·73	3·89	4·12	4·47	5·10	6·55
	0·01	3·36	3·78	4·16	4·30	4·50	4·64	4·82	5·06	5·41	5·95	6·93	9·33
14	0·05	2·13	2·35	2·53	2·60	2·70	2·76	2·85	2·96	3·11	3·34	3·74	4·60
	0·025	2·49	2·79	3·05	3·15	3·29	3·38	3·50	3·66	3·89	4·24	4·86	6·30
	0·01	3·00	3·43	3·80	3·94	4·14	4·28	4·46	4·70	5·04	5·56	6·51	8·86
16	0·05	2·01	2·24	2·42	2·49	2·59	2·66	2·74	2·85	3·01	3·24	3·63	4·49
	0·025	2·32	2·63	2·89	2·99	3·12	3·22	3·34	3·50	3·73	4·08	4·69	6·12
	0·01	2·75	3·18	3·55	3·69	3·89	4·03	4·20	4·44	4·77	5·29	6·23	8·53
18	0·05	1·92	2·15	2·34	2·41	2·51	2·58	2·66	2·77	2·93	3·16	3·55	4·41
	0·025	2·19	2·50	2·77	2·87	3·01	3·10	3·22	3·38	3·61	3·95	4·56	5·98
	0·01	2·57	3·00	3·37	3·51	3·71	3·84	4·01	4·25	4·58	5·09	6·01	8·29
20	0·05	1·84	2·08	2·28	2·35	2·45	2·51	2·60	2·71	2·87	3·10	3·49	4·35
	0·025	2·02	2·41	2·68	2·77	2·91	3·01	3·13	3·29	3·51	3·86	4·46	5·87
	0·01	2·49	2·86	3·23	3·37	3·56	3·70	3·87	4·10	4·43	4·94	5·85	8·10

Probability of exceeding F	v_2	v_1 = 1	2	3	4	5	6	7	8	10	12	24	∞
0·05	24	4·26	3·40	3·01	2·78	2·62	2·51	2·42	2·36	2·25	2·18	1·98	1·73
0·025		5·72	4·32	3·72	3·38	3·15	2·99	2·87	2·78	2·64	2·54	2·27	1·94
0·01		7·82	5·61	4·72	4·22	3·90	3·67	3·50	3·36	3·17	3·03	2·66	2·21
0·05	28	4·20	3·34	2·95	2·71	2·56	2·45	2·36	2·29	2·19	2·12	1·91	1·65
0·025		5·61	4·22	3·63	3·29	3·06	2·90	2·78	2·69	2·55	2·45	2·17	1·83
0·01		7·64	5·45	4·57	4·07	3·75	3·53	3·36	3·23	3·03	2·90	2·52	2·06
0·05	32	4·15	3·29	2·90	2·67	2·51	2·40	2·31	2·24	2·14	2·07	1·86	1·59
0·025		5·53	4·15	3·56	3·22	3·00	2·84	2·72	2·62	2·48	2·38	2·10	1·75
0·01		7·50	5·34	4·46	3·97	3·65	3·43	3·26	3·13	2·93	2·80	2·42	1·96
0·05	36	4·11	3·26	2·87	2·63	2·48	2·36	2·28	2·21	2·11	2·03	1·82	1·55
0·025		5·47	4·09	3·51	3·17	2·94	2·79	2·66	2·57	2·43	2·33	2·05	1·69
0·01		7·40	5·25	4·38	3·89	3·58	3·35	3·18	3·05	2·86	2·72	2·35	1·87
0·05	40	4·08	3·23	2·84	2·61	2·45	2·34	2·25	2·18	2·08	2·00	1·79	1·51
0·025		5·42	4·05	3·46	3·13	2·90	2·74	2·62	2·53	2·39	2·29	2·01	1·64
0·01		7·31	5·18	4·31	3·83	3·51	3·29	3·12	2·99	2·80	2·66	2·29	1·80
0·05	60	4·00	3·15	2·76	2·53	2·37	2·25	2·17	2·10	1·99	1·92	1·70	1·39
0·025		5·29	3·93	3·34	3·01	2·79	2·63	2·51	2·41	2·27	2·17	1·88	1·48
0·01		7·08	4·98	4·13	3·65	3·34	3·12	2·95	2·82	2·63	2·50	2·12	1·60
0·05	120	3·92	3·07	2·68	2·45	2·29	2·18	2·09	2·02	1·91	1·83	1·61	1·25
0·025		5·15	3·80	3·23	2·89	2·67	2·52	2·39	2·30	2·16	2·05	1·76	1·31
0·01		6·85	4·79	3·95	3·48	3·17	2·96	2·79	2·66	2·47	2·34	1·95	1·38
0·05	∞	3·84	3·00	2·60	2·37	2·21	2·10	2·01	1·94	1·83	1·75	1·52	1·00
0·025		5·02	3·69	3·12	2·79	2·57	2·41	2·29	2·19	2·05	1·94	1·64	1·00
0·01		6·63	4·61	3·78	3·32	3·02	2·80	2·64	2·51	2·32	2·18	1·79	1·00

Table A4 Correlation coefficient

Shaded area $Q = Q_1 + Q_2$ is the probability that a value of $|r|$ calculated with ν degrees of freedom will exceed $|r_Q|$ for completely uncorrelated data (see section 6.2.3).

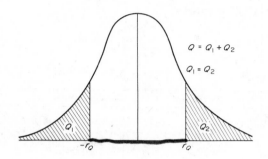

	Probability of exceeding the magnitude of r		
ν	$0 \cdot 1$	$0 \cdot 05$	$0 \cdot 01$
1	0·98769	0·99692	0·999877
2	0·90000	0·95000	0·990000
3	0·8054	0·8783	0·95873
4	0·7293	0·8114	0·91720
5	0·6694	0·7545	0·8745
6	0·6215	0·7067	0·8343
7	0·5822	0·6664	0·7977
8	0·5494	0·6319	0·7646
9	0·5214	0·6021	0·7348
10	0·4973	0·5760	0·7079
11	0·4762	0·5529	0·6835
12	0·4575	0·5324	0·6614
13	0·4409	0·5139	0·6411
14	0·4259	0·4973	0·6226
15	0·4124	0·4821	0·6055
16	0·4000	0·4683	0·5897
17	0·3887	0·4555	0·5751
18	0·3783	0·4438	0·5614
19	0·3687	0·4329	0·5487
20	0·3598	0·4227	0·5368
25	0·3233	0·3809	0·4869
30	0·2960	0·3494	0·4487
35	0·2746	0·3246	0·4182
40	0·2573	0·3044	0·3932
45	0·2428	0·2875	0·3721
50	0·2306	0·2732	0·3541
60	0·2108	0·2500	0·3248
70	0·1954	0·2319	0·3017
80	0·1829	0·2172	0·2830
90	0·1726	0·2050	0·2673
100	0·1638	0·1946	0·2540

Table A5 Chi-squared distribution

Shaded area Q is the probability that a value of χ^2 calculated with ν degrees of freedom will exceed χ^2_Q if the observed and expected values will have the same distribution (see section 9.3).

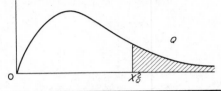

ν	Probability of Deviation greater than χ^2					
	$0 \cdot 99$	$0 \cdot 975$	$0 \cdot 95$	$0 \cdot 05$	$0 \cdot 025$	$0 \cdot 01$
1	$0 \cdot 000157$	$0 \cdot 000982$	$0 \cdot 00393$	$3 \cdot 84$	$5 \cdot 02$	$6 \cdot 63$
2	$0 \cdot 0201$	$0 \cdot 0506$	$0 \cdot 103$	$5 \cdot 99$	$7 \cdot 38$	$9 \cdot 21$
3	$0 \cdot 115$	$0 \cdot 216$	$0 \cdot 352$	$7 \cdot 81$	$9 \cdot 35$	$11 \cdot 34$
4	$0 \cdot 297$	$0 \cdot 484$	$0 \cdot 711$	$9 \cdot 49$	$11 \cdot 14$	$13 \cdot 28$
5	$0 \cdot 554$	$0 \cdot 831$	$1 \cdot 15$	$11 \cdot 07$	$12 \cdot 83$	$15 \cdot 09$
6	$0 \cdot 872$	$1 \cdot 24$	$1 \cdot 64$	$12 \cdot 59$	$14 \cdot 45$	$16 \cdot 81$
7	$1 \cdot 24$	$1 \cdot 69$	$2 \cdot 17$	$14 \cdot 07$	$16 \cdot 01$	$18 \cdot 48$
8	$1 \cdot 65$	$2 \cdot 18$	$2 \cdot 73$	$15 \cdot 51$	$17 \cdot 53$	$20 \cdot 09$
9	$2 \cdot 09$	$2 \cdot 70$	$3 \cdot 33$	$16 \cdot 92$	$19 \cdot 02$	$21 \cdot 67$
10	$2 \cdot 56$	$3 \cdot 25$	$3 \cdot 94$	$18 \cdot 31$	$20 \cdot 48$	$23 \cdot 21$
11	$3 \cdot 05$	$3 \cdot 82$	$4 \cdot 57$	$19 \cdot 68$	$21 \cdot 92$	$24 \cdot 73$
12	$3 \cdot 57$	$4 \cdot 40$	$5 \cdot 23$	$21 \cdot 03$	$23 \cdot 34$	$26 \cdot 22$
13	$4 \cdot 11$	$5 \cdot 01$	$5 \cdot 89$	$22 \cdot 36$	$24 \cdot 74$	$27 \cdot 69$
14	$4 \cdot 66$	$5 \cdot 63$	$6 \cdot 57$	$23 \cdot 68$	$26 \cdot 12$	$29 \cdot 14$
15	$5 \cdot 23$	$6 \cdot 26$	$7 \cdot 26$	$25 \cdot 00$	$27 \cdot 49$	$30 \cdot 58$
16	$5 \cdot 81$	$6 \cdot 91$	$7 \cdot 96$	$26 \cdot 30$	$28 \cdot 85$	$32 \cdot 00$
17	$6 \cdot 41$	$7 \cdot 56$	$8 \cdot 67$	$27 \cdot 59$	$30 \cdot 19$	$33 \cdot 41$
18	$7 \cdot 01$	$8 \cdot 23$	$9 \cdot 39$	$28 \cdot 87$	$31 \cdot 53$	$34 \cdot 81$
19	$7 \cdot 63$	$8 \cdot 91$	$10 \cdot 12$	$30 \cdot 14$	$32 \cdot 85$	$36 \cdot 19$
20	$8 \cdot 26$	$9 \cdot 59$	$10 \cdot 85$	$31 \cdot 41$	$34 \cdot 17$	$37 \cdot 57$
21	$8 \cdot 90$	$10 \cdot 28$	$11 \cdot 59$	$32 \cdot 67$	$35 \cdot 48$	$38 \cdot 93$
22	$9 \cdot 54$	$10 \cdot 98$	$12 \cdot 34$	$33 \cdot 92$	$36 \cdot 78$	$40 \cdot 29$
23	$10 \cdot 20$	$11 \cdot 69$	$13 \cdot 09$	$35 \cdot 17$	$38 \cdot 08$	$41 \cdot 64$
24	$10 \cdot 86$	$12 \cdot 40$	$13 \cdot 85$	$36 \cdot 42$	$39 \cdot 36$	$42 \cdot 98$
25	$11 \cdot 52$	$13 \cdot 12$	$14 \cdot 61$	$37 \cdot 65$	$40 \cdot 65$	$44 \cdot 31$
26	$12 \cdot 20$	$13 \cdot 84$	$15 \cdot 38$	$38 \cdot 89$	$41 \cdot 92$	$45 \cdot 64$
27	$12 \cdot 88$	$14 \cdot 57$	$16 \cdot 15$	$40 \cdot 11$	$43 \cdot 19$	$46 \cdot 96$
28	$13 \cdot 56$	$15 \cdot 31$	$16 \cdot 93$	$41 \cdot 34$	$44 \cdot 46$	$48 \cdot 28$
29	$14 \cdot 26$	$16 \cdot 05$	$17 \cdot 71$	$42 \cdot 56$	$45 \cdot 72$	$49 \cdot 59$
30	$14 \cdot 95$	$16 \cdot 79$	$18 \cdot 49$	$43 \cdot 77$	$46 \cdot 98$	$50 \cdot 89$
40	$22 \cdot 16$	$24 \cdot 43$	$26 \cdot 51$	$55 \cdot 76$	$59 \cdot 34$	$63 \cdot 69$
50	$29 \cdot 71$	$32 \cdot 36$	$34 \cdot 76$	$67 \cdot 50$	$71 \cdot 42$	$76 \cdot 15$
60	$37 \cdot 48$	$40 \cdot 48$	$43 \cdot 19$	$79 \cdot 08$	$83 \cdot 30$	$88 \cdot 38$
70	$45 \cdot 44$	$48 \cdot 76$	$51 \cdot 74$	$90 \cdot 53$	$95 \cdot 02$	$100 \cdot 4$
80	$53 \cdot 54$	$57 \cdot 15$	$60 \cdot 39$	$101 \cdot 9$	$106 \cdot 6$	$112 \cdot 3$
90	$61 \cdot 75$	$65 \cdot 65$	$69 \cdot 13$	$113 \cdot 1$	$118 \cdot 1$	$124 \cdot 1$
100	$70 \cdot 06$	$74 \cdot 22$	$77 \cdot 93$	$124 \cdot 3$	$129 \cdot 6$	$135 \cdot 8$

For large values of ν, $\sqrt{2\chi^2}$ is approximately normally distributed with mean $\sqrt{2\nu - 1}$ and unit variance.

Table A6. Median, 5 per cent and 95 per cent ranks for up to ten items

					Sample size n					
j*	1	2	3	4	5	6	7	8	9	10
1	.5000	.2929	.2063	.1591	.1294	.1091	.0943	.0830	.0741	.0670
2		.7071	.5000	.3864	.3147	.2655	.2295	.2021	.1806	.1632
3			.7937	.6136	.5000	.4218	.3648	.3213	.2871	.2594
4				.8409	.6853	.5782	.5000	.4404	.3935	.3557
5					.8706	.7345	.6352	.5596	.5000	.4519
6						.8909	.7705	.6787	.6065	.5481
7							.9057	.7979	.7129	.6443
8								.9170	.8194	.7406
9									.9259	.8368
10										.9330

Median ranks

					Sample size n					
j*	1	2	3	4	5	6	7	8	9	10
1	.0500	.0253	.0170	.0127	.0102	.0085	.0074	.0065	.0057	.0051
2		.2236	.1354	.0976	.0764	.0629	.0534	.0468	.0410	.0368
3			.3684	.2486	.1893	.1532	.1287	.1111	.0978	.0873
4				.4729	.3426	.2713	.2253	.1929	.1688	.1500
5					.5493	.4182	.3413	.2892	.2514	.2224
6						.6070	.4793	.4003	.3449	.3035
7							.6518	.5293	.4504	.3934
8								.6877	.5709	.4931
9									.7169	.6058
10										.7411

5 per cent ranks

					Sample size n					
j*	1	2	3	4	5	6	7	8	9	10
1	.9500	.7764	.6316	.5271	.4507	.3930	.3482	.3123	.2831	.2589
2		.9747	.8646	.7514	.6574	.5818	.5207	.4707	.4291	.3942
3			.9830	.9024	.8107	.7287	.6587	.5997	.5496	.5069
4				.9873	.9236	.8468	.7747	.7108	.6551	.6076
5					.9898	.9371	.8713	.8071	.7436	.6965
6						.9915	.9466	.8889	.8312	.7776
7							.9926	.9532	.9032	.8500
8								.9935	.9590	.9127
9									.9943	.9632
10										.9949

95 per cent ranks

Index